ACTIVATE YOUR VAGUS NERVE

Stimulate And Activate The Natural Healing Power Of Vagus Nerve With Self-Help Exercises For Anxiety, And Panic Attacks. Relieve Depression, Ptsd And Chronic Illness Today

By
Mike Malone

© Copyright 2021 by Mike Malone - All rights reserved.

The following Book is reproduced below with the goal of providing information that is as accurate and reliable as possible. Regardless, purchasing this Book can be seen as consent to the fact that both the publisher and the author of this book are in no way experts on the topics discussed within and that any recommendations or suggestions that are made herein are for entertainment purposes only. Professionals should be consulted as needed prior to undertaking any of the action endorsed herein.

This declaration is deemed fair and valid by both the American Bar Association and the Committee of Publishers Association and is legally binding throughout the United States.

Furthermore, the transmission, duplication, or reproduction of any of the following work including specific information will be considered an illegal act irrespective of if it is done electronically or in print. This extends to creating a secondary or tertiary copy of the work or a recorded copy and is only allowed with the express written consent from the Publisher. All additional right reserved.

The information in the following pages is broadly considered a truthful and accurate account of facts and as such, any inattention, use, or misuse of the information in question by the reader will render any resulting actions solely under their purview. There are no scenarios in which the publisher or the original author of this work can be in any fashion deemed liable for any hardship or damages that may befall them after undertaking information described herein.

Additionally, the information in the following pages is intended only for informational purposes and should thus be thought of as universal. As befitting its nature, it is presented without assurance regarding its prolonged validity or interim quality. Trademarks that are mentioned are done without written consent and can in no way be considered an endorsement from the trademark holder.

Table of Contents

INTRODUCTION 6

WHAT IS VAGUS NERVE AND WHERE IS IT? 11
    THE STRUCTURE OF THE VAGUS NERVE 12
    THE FUNCTIONS OF THE VAGUS NERVE 16

HOW TO ACTIVATE AND ACCESS THE POWER OF THE VAGUS NERVE 29
    MEASURING VAGUS NERVE FUNCTION 37
    DIAPHRAGMATIC BREATHING 42
    AUDIBLE BREATHING 44
    OBSTRUCTED DIAPHRAGMATIC BREATHING EXERCISE 45
    PHYSICAL EXERCISES 46
    WALKING 46
    HIGH-INTENSITY INTERVAL SPRINTING 47
    CARDIO MACHINES 47
    JUMP ROPE 48

INFLAMMATION, AND DISEASES ASSOCIATED WITH VAGUS NERVE 49
    WHAT IS INFLAMMATION? 50

THE BENEFITS OF VAGUS NERVE STIMULATION 64
    VAGAL TONE 68
    VAGUS NERVE STIMULATION 70
    CARDIOVASCULAR HEALTH 75
    PREVENTION OF INFLAMMATION 76
    BREATHING 77
    IMPROVED MEMORY 78
    WEIGHT MANAGEMENT 78
    STRESS MANAGEMENT 79
    GUT FEELINGS 80

UNDERSTANDING PTSD, TRAUMA 81
    WHAT IS TRAUMA? 82
    TYPES OF TRAUMA 83
    WHAT IS PTSD? 87
    VAGUS NERVE EXERCISES THAT CAN HELP INDIVIDUALS OVERCOME PTSD AND TRAUMA 94

VAGUS NERVE AND ANXIETY DISORDER 99

    History Of Anxiety Disorders 100
    Types Of Anxiety Disorders 103
    Major Causes Of Anxiety Disorders 112

BODY AND MIND CONNECTION 118

THE NATURAL HEALING POWER OF YOUR BODY WITH SELF-HELP EXERCISES AND TECHNIQUES 135

    Exercise 136
    Speed Walking 140
    Stretching 141
    Yoga For Chronic Pain 142
    Massage Therapy 146
    Brain Balance 151
    Emotional Freedom Techniques 154

STEP BY STEP INSTRUCTIONS TO STRENGTHEN YOUR VAGUS NERVE TO UPGRADE YOUR WHOLE BODY 156

CONCLUSION 175

Introduction

You need your nerves. That much is certain. When your nerves function well, your whole body becomes capable of becoming the well-oiled machine it needs to be. The vagus nerve, however, becomes a sort of commander of most of your organs. As a cranial nerve, your vagus nerve has a very special function— it can take stimulation from your body straight to the brain without it having to go through alternate pathways. If you were to imagine all your nerves existing as a sort of transit system, complete with all sorts of stops along the way, your cranial nerves would be like the express routes. They get you from point A to B without having to go between other intermediaries. While other signals throughout your body will route back through your spinal cord, your vagus nerve is a direct line of travel from the body to the brain.

We are going to be discussing the vagus nerve, learning how it works and what you can expect from it. When you understand how your vagus nerve works and why it matters, you can begin to identify the areas in which your life may have been impacted by it in some way. You may be surprised to find out that, all along, you had a low vagal tone, implying that your vagus nerve is not firing properly. Your vagal tone is the way in which we determine how functional that vagus nerve is. While it can be checked through directly connecting to the vagus nerve to identify just how much activity is occurring within it, there are other methods that you can use as well. You can discover the health of your vagus nerve through the variation in your heart rate during your inhales and exhales. When there is a larger variation between the inhale and exhale, it is believed that the vagus nerve is more powerful—it is referred to as toned. When you see very little variability, however, you may have other secondary problems occurring as well, and that is when you want to start considering interventions to help support it.

The vagus nerve is a pair of cranial nerves that originate from the base of the brainstem. They travel down from the brainstem in several different branches that reach across much of the body. This nerve is named vagus from the same root word of vagabond—it means wanderer. Aptly named, the vagus nerve travels throughout the face, the neck, the torso, and the abdomen, innervating several different areas and influencing how they work.

In particular, the vagus nerve is sensorimotor. This means that, while most nerves are specialized one way or the other, the vagus nerve has the capability to communicate both to and from the brain. It allows for sensation and sensory data to be taken to the brain, which is where the afferent nature comes into play. However, it also sends commands from the brain to the rest of the body to control it, which is where it gets its efferent ability. It can not only sense but moves the body around you.

As a rule, if you need to remember between afferent and efferent, try using this quick mnemonic: afferent nerves arrive at the brain with their information while efferent nerves exit the brain with their information. Afferent nerves are your sensory nerves that would need to be able to send information straight to the brain in order to have it processed properly. Efferent nerves are your motor nerves that are responsible for moving your muscles and controlling your body, even if the muscles that are being moved are the involuntary muscles of your organs that keep you alive.

This nerve, however, is important just since it is so widely reaching and due to the wide range of the control it has over the body. It is intricately involved in your emotional regulation, determining how you handle stress and how you interact with other people. It is responsible for ensuring that you are capable of functioning thanks to the intermediary that it plays between all these important body parts and the brain.

You can see the vagus nerve serving as a sort of regulator of the autonomic nervous system. It allows for the fear responses that people have. That fear response is what the body needs to be ready and able to interact with the world. Think about it—if you had to consciously consider the pros and cons of running away from a tiger instead of fighting the tiger off, there is a good chance that you would spend so much time deliberating between the two that instead, you would wind up getting attacked long before you made a decision. Because of that, the vagus nerve takes control for you. It makes these sorts of snap-decisions for you, so you do not have to make them instead. It removes that delay of having to consciously decide what you do so you can react instinctively. You respond with that same primal part of your brain that will lead other animals to react to their surroundings. You will usually either fight, run away, or freeze up altogether, but it happens without you making the decision yourself in order to save you crucial time that will otherwise be better spent keeping you alive.

What is Vagus Nerve and Where is it?

The vagus nerve is the longest of the cranial nerves and is functionally one of the most important nerves in the body. Heart rate, digestion, blood pressure, sweating, and even vocal function are some of the vital physiological processes that are regulated by the vagus nerve. It is the main link for the transmission of information between the brain and other body organs and tissues. The vagus nerve, therefore, facilitates the monitoring of various organ systems by the brain.

The Structure Of The Vagus Nerve

The Vagus Nerve derives its name from the Latin term vagary that alludes to its wandering and long structure that extends from the head to the abdomen. It is the longest and most complex of the 12 cranial nerves. It travels through the jugular foramen, passes into the carotid sheath between the internal carotid artery and the internal jugular vein below the head, to the neck, chest, and abdomen, where it facilitates the innervation of the viscera.

From the medulla of the brain stream, the vagus nerve exits the cranium through the jugular foramen, which is in the base of the skull. Within the skull, the auricular branch of the Vagus nerve arises to provide a sensory response to the auditory canal as well as the external ear. From the head, the vagus nerve then extends to the neck through the carotid sheath.

The vagus nerve, while in the neck will travel inferiorly with the jugular vein and the carotid until the base of the neck at which point the right and left vagus nerve branch into two different pathways. The right vagus nerve enters the thorax by passing anteriorly to the subclavian artery and posteriorly to the sternoclavicular joint. In contrast, the left vagus nerve will enter the thorax, passing posteriorly to the sternoclavicular joint and between the carotid and left subclavian arteries.

While in the neck the Vagus nerve branches into;

- The superior laryngeal nerve consisting of internal and external branches. The external branch of the laryngeal nerve provides sensory innervation for the larynx through the cricothyroid muscle.
- The pharyngeal branch which provides motor innervation to muscles of the soft palate and pharynx.
- The recurrent laryngeal nerve extends from the right subclavian artery to the larynx and function in innervating the muscles of the larynx.

Once the vagus nerve gets to the chest, it branches into the posterior vagal trunk and the anterior vagal trunk. The anterior vagal trunk arises from the left vagus nerve, while the posterior vagal trunk arises from the right vagus nerve. The smooth muscles of the esophagus are innervated by the esophageal plexus, which is formed by these vagal trunks.

The cardiac branches which also arise in the thorax function in the innervation of the heart muscles regulating the heart rate. Most of the muscles of the larynx are innervated by the left recurrent laryngeal nerve. The vagal trunks from the thorax extend to the abdomen through an opening in the diaphragm, referred to as the esophageal hiatus.

While in the abdomen, the vagal trunks divide into multiple branches that supply the small and large bowels, the stomach, and the esophagus.

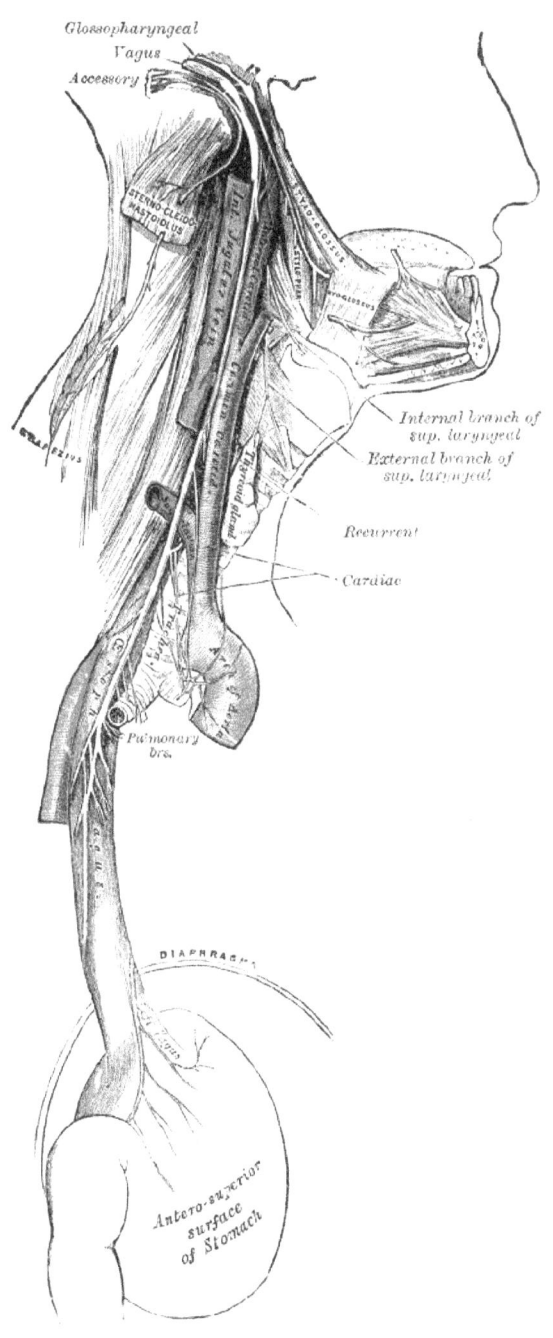

The Functions Of The Vagus Nerve

The vagus nerve is a mixed cranial nerve that has both sensory and motor functions. The sensory functions of the vagus nerve can be either somatic or visceral in nature. Sensations felt on the skin or in the muscles are typically somatic, while those felt in the body organs are visceral.

The sensory functions of the Vagus nerve include;

- Supplying visceral sensation to the heart, lungs, digestive system, trachea, esophagus, and the larynx.
- Providing somatic sensation to parts of the throat and the ear canal.
- The sensation of taste at the base of the tongue

The motor functions of the vagus nerve include;

- The vagus nerve innervates heart muscles, thereby regulating the heart rate.
- The vagus nerve facilitates peristalsis or the movement of food through the digestive tract by stimulating contractions in the esophagus, stomach, and in the intestines.
- The vagus nerve stimulates muscles in the larynx, pharynx, and the soft palate.

The greatest significance of the vagus nerve when it comes to health is that it is the body's major parasympathetic nerve. This means that it supplies parasympathetic fibers to all the major organs in the head, neck, and chest, as well as the abdomen.

The vagus nerve is responsible for involuntary parasympathetic responses and is in control of functions such as the gag reflex, sneezing, and coughing reflexes. Afferent vagus nerve fibers that stimulate the pharynx and back of the throat stimulate the gag reflex. In fact, doctors will often check vagal activity by testing the gag reflex by tickling the back of the throat with a soft cotton swab, if this test fails to elicit gagging in the patient; it serves as an indicator of vagus nerve dysfunction.

Other physiological functions that are regulated by the vagus nerve include; slowing down the heart rate, regulating sweating, controlling blood pressure, and even peristalsis, which is the movement of food in the gastrointestinal tract to facilitate digestion.

By creating a crucial link for the brain to organ and organ to brain communication, the vagus nerve enables the brain to regulate different processes and organ functions to ensure that the body is maintained in the ideal homeostatic state. For our organs to function properly, processes need to be inhibited or activated depending on our internal or external environment.

Take, for instance, a person who is jogging. Their energy demands will be high in order to sustain physical activity. This will require the heart to beat faster, pumping more blood to the muscles so that they get enough oxygen. Now let's consider someone who is taking a nap, their energy demand is low since the body is in a rested state, and hence their heart rate will be slower because the energy demand by the body is low.

In effect, your body needs to adjust to your internal and external state appropriately to the internal and external environment in order to remain in optimum health. The vagus nerve plays an important afferent role by bringing information from the internal organs such as the heart, lungs, and gut to the brain. Moreover, it also functions in an efferent role where it mitigates the effects of the sympathetic nervous system.

The vagus nerve in its parasympathetic role is a big determinant of how well the internal homeostasis or balance in the body is maintained. The fight and flight responses that are activated by the sympathetic system during times of stress or danger need to be effectively switched off or inhibited once the threat has been resolved; this is where the parasympathetic role of the vagus nerve comes in.

As we have seen, fight or flight responses are our bodies' way of preparing us to fight threats. Without these responses, our lives would be short because we would not have adequate self-defense mechanisms. Look at it this way, without the adrenaline rush that comes with fear. You may not be able to outrun that aggressive dog or fight off an aggressor. By increasing your energy reserves by elevating your heart rate, breathing rate, and even reducing your sensitivity to pain, the fight and flight responses enable you to defend yourself from threats.

However, what happens after the threat has been resolved, and you are no longer in danger? Your body needs to return to a rested state for normal body function to resume. This is achieved when the vagus nerve in its parasympathetic role inhibits the fight and flight responses and restores the body to a rested state.

The vagus nerve effectively puts the body back in a relaxed or rested state by slowing down the heartbeat, decreasing the rate of respiration, and stimulating digestive function. These interventions by the vagus nerve ensure that once a threat has been resolved, your body is reverted to a relaxed and rested state.

Without the proper functioning of the vagus nerve, the sympathetic nervous system becomes overstimulated, and this, in turn, causes disorders in the body. To ensure that our vagal activity is high, there are measures we can take to routinely stimulate and activate its parasympathetic effects and ensure that we reap the benefits of the healing power of this powerful nerve.

The Vagus Nerve and Good Health

While we can understand the functions of the vagus nerve in the body, it is even more important to relate these functions to our physical and mental health and understand the role of the vagus nerve in maintaining physical and psychological health.

Cardiovascular Health

The vagus nerve plays a crucial role in ensuring normal cardiovascular function. The vagus nerve regulates the heart rate in effect functioning as a natural pacemaker. By stimulating the cardiac muscles, the vagus nerve can effectively slow down our heart rate when it is too fast, as happens in stressful conditions. When the heart rate is increased, it can lead to the elevation of the blood pressure, which causes strain on the heart tissue and blood vessels.

Research has shown that a decrease in vagal activity or vagal tone is linked to an increase in mortality when it comes to heart failure conditions. By regulating the heart rate, the vagus nerve can effectively reduce blood pressure and by extension, reduces damage to the cardiac muscles. A properly functioning vagus nerve is, therefore, crucial for cardiovascular health and in avoiding conditions such as hypertension.

Chronic Inflammation

Have you ever noticed that redness, swelling, or even pus that occurs when you injure yourself? Notice how, when you fall and scrape your knees or stub your toe, the affected area becomes swollen and red? These are all indicators of inflammation that we routinely experience.

Inflammation is an essential part of the immune system's reaction to physical injury or pathogenic infection in the body. Inflammation signals the immune system to heal and repair injured tissue and defend itself against pathogens such as bacteria and other disease-causing pathogens. Without inflammation as a defense mechanism, wounds would not heal, and even minor infections could prove fatal.

On the flip side, when an inflammatory response is prolonged for extended periods of time, the body begins to attack its cells. This is referred to as chronic inflammation. In fact, chronic inflammation is an underlying cause in diseases such as heart disease, stroke, and autoimmune disorders, including rheumatoid arthritis and lupus.

What this means is that while inflammation is a natural part of the healing process, when it goes on uninhibited for extended periods of time, it can cause severe health problems. The vagus nerve becomes instrumental in managing chronic inflammation because of its parasympathetic responses that can effectively inhibit the sympathetic responses of fight or flight. When your vagal activity or tone is strong, the vagus nerve can effectively inhibit inflammatory responses and prevent overstimulation of the immune system.

On the other hand, a reduced vagal tone results in the secretion of pro-inflammatory cytokines and ultimately causes an increase in sympathetic nervous system responses that are linked to chronic inflammation.

The vagus nerve can effectively control inflammation by inhibiting the overstimulation of the immune system that is caused by the sympathetic nervous system. Medical research has shown that stimulation of the vagus nerve helps in managing conditions that are related to prolonged inflammation of tissues in the body. Vagal stimulation has been found to be effective as a therapy in managing pain in rheumatoid arthritis and other autoimmune disorders.

Weight Management

Ever wondered where some people could feel full after eating only a small portion of food while others take longer to feel satiated? Well, this phenomenon is linked to the sensitivity of the vagus nerve. The more sensitive your vagus nerve is, the quicker you feel full when eating, and the lower the sensitivity of the vagus nerve, the longer it will take you to feel full.

But how does this come about? The answer lies in the gut-brain axis, which is the connection between the brain and the gut. The link and communication between these two organs are facilitated by the vagus nerve. The vagus nerve is the main communication channel between the gastrointestinal tract and the brain. This means that the efficacy of the vagus nerve function will have an impact on various factors, including:

- Digestion
- Weight gain or weight loss

In a scenario where the vagal tone is decreased, it loses the sensitivity that enables it to detect and communicate to the brain that the stomach is full. The net result of this is overeating, which inevitably leads to weight gain and digestive disorders.

An increased vagal tone means that the vagus nerve will have a higher sensitivity to the fullness signal from the gut, and this means that you will tend to feel full faster and on less food. This is essential in weight management because most people struggling with weight management tend to consume more calories than the body requires. Therefore, the less you eat, the easier it is to keep the excess pounds off.

Stress Management

Stress is one of the leading causes of ill health in the world today. From physical to psychological disorders, stress is a major underlying cause of poor health. When we think of fight and flight responses, it is easy to assume that they are only triggered by physical threats. This is not true. Whether your stress is emotional or physical, the body's response is to activate the fight or flight mode to enable you to resolve the imminent threat or stress factor.

When you are anxious about work, worrying about your children, or even fretting about the daily pressures of life, your sympathetic nervous system perceives a threat and triggers the fight or flight response. This means that when you are dealing with chronic stress or anxiety, the flight or fight responses are perpetually turned on. This, as we have seen, can lead to chronic inflammation, autoimmune disorders, and a myriad of health complications.

Since the vagus nerve can effectively inhibit the fight or flight responses, it can easily restore the body to a rest and relaxed state. This means that it will counteract the fight or flight responses, such as the release of cortisol, which has been linked to weight, gain, insomnia, and even hypertension. The vagus nerve helps in combating stress because it can stop the fight and flight responses that are triggered when you are stressed, anxious, or in danger.

A common technique used in managing anxiety and even anger is taking slow and deep breaths. The mechanism behind this is that deep breathing activates the vagus nerve and enables it to restore the body to a relaxed and rested state. This is crucial when it comes to stress management. People with poor vagal activity are prone to chronic stress and depressive tendencies because their fight and flight response system are not being sufficiently kept in check by the vagus nerve.

Proper Breathing

One of the effects of Vagus nerve activity is in controlling our respiration rate through its effect on the bronchioles. The Vagus nerve facilitates proper breathing through the neurotransmitter acetylcholine. Proper breathing is not only an effective way to deal with pain but is also effective in coping with stress by creating a calming effect on the body.

Since the vagus nerve is connected to the diaphragm, it is possible to stimulate it by doing deep abdominal breathing or holding your breath for six to seven counts. Relaxation techniques such as meditation and yoga incorporate breathing techniques because proper breathing has a relaxing effect on the body.

Improved memory

Stimulation of the vagus nerve has been found to affect improving memory and cognitive ability. When the vagus nerve is stimulated, it triggers the release of the neurotransmitter norepinephrine into the amygdala, which forms part of the limbic system. This means that the activation of the vagus nerve can be beneficial in counteracting and managing the effects of some cognitive disorders such as Alzheimer's.

How to Activate and Access the Power of the Vagus Nerve

Simulating the vagus nerve can be a bit more difficult than it sounds. This nerve runs through almost every major organ, from the brain to the colon (Roland, 2019).

Many of the techniques for stimulating the vagus nerve requires one's full body. Yoga, for example, is an amazing way to stimulate the vagus nerve. Not only does it soothe and calm almost all the major organs, but positions that stretch the spine and neck directly stimulate the nerve itself (Spindler, 2018). The lungs and heart are both healed and soothed by the deep breathing and physical activity of yoga (Spindler, 2018).

You can think about vagus nerve healing as physical, mental, emotional, or even spiritual. Spiritual practices like meditation stimulate the nerve just as readily as more physical activities. Regardless of your own spiritual beliefs, ideas about positive and negative energy, mindfulness, and interconnectedness have a great deal of validity when we look at how the vagus nerve works. Whether you want to think about these exercises as improving the neurological functions of the nerve or allowing positive energy to flow through the body, the result (and the basic underlying idea) is the same.

Different exercises will work for different people. Everyone is trying to heal, recover, or prevent something different. However, I encourage you to try each of these exercises at least once, no matter how strange or unrelated to your healing journey they may seem. It may seem "new age" to think that something like sound healing or aromatherapy could help you to manage something cancer or MS, but you might be amazed by how much better you feel.

Most of the exercises given in this chapter will be things that you can do at home, or without the help of a professional. However, there are many therapies and techniques that require the intervention of a licensed professional that will also stimulate the vagus nerve. There are also some therapies that you can choose to do by yourself or with a professional. Yoga, for example, is something you can do at home with a book or following a YouTube channel. Or you can find a local studio and take classes with a licensed professional. The choice is yours!

However, as a reference, here is a more complete list of activities that can help you to stimulate the vagus nerve, sorted into the four healing categories of physical, mental, emotional, and spiritual. All of us will naturally gravitate to one of these four healing techniques. Of the four may seem most appropriate for your own healing journey. This is perfectly natural. However, I do encourage you to try at least one technique from all four categories to begin approaching your health and wellness from a more holistic place.

Physical (Atkinson, 2019)

- Exercise

- Speed walking
- Stretching
- Yoga
- Massage therapies
- Detoxification
- Activated charcoal
- Skin brushing and saunas
- Gallbladder flush
- Herbs and herbal supplements
- Eating plant-based, whole foods
- Drinking water
- Nutritional supplements
- Limit alcohol
- Limit caffeine
- Hot baths

- Cold showers
- Go outside
- Get enough sleep
- Aromatherapy

Mental (Psychological) (Atkinson, 2019)

- Affirmations
- Brain balance
- Visualizations and goal setting
- Biofeedback
- Journaling
- Talk therapy
- Cognitive behavioral therapy
- Psychotherapy
- Limit social media engagement
- Positive social interactions

- Hobbies or activities that are purely done for fun

Emotional

- Listening to and/or playing music
- Emotional freedom techniques
- Cultivate a positive attitude
- Self-comforting techniques
- Letting go
- Relaxation techniques
- Practicing gratitude
- Self-rewarding
- Decompression
- Grounding techniques
- Hypnosis
- Lifestyle changes to eliminate negative people or situations

Spiritual

- Yoga

- Sound healing

- Biofeedback

- Meditation

- Mindfulness

- Aromatherapy

- Spiritual healing (of any religious or spiritual belief)

- Crystal healing

- Prayer or spiritual ritual

- Chakra healing

    - Connecting with nature

Many of these techniques seem simple, even too simple. But remember how the vagus nerve works. Polyvagal theory teaches us that the vagus nerve shuts down when it perceives that we are in danger. It begins to fire different signals to ensure that we survive whatever is threatening our safety. However, when our bodies are chronically in the danger state, the vagus nerve remains dysfunctional for long periods of time, and we never enter the state of recovery and healing that necessarily follows a period of danger. Every exercise or technique that stimulates the vagus nerve is meant to bring your body out of the danger state, which means convincing the body and/or mind that you are in a place of safety.

If you have multiple illnesses, it will take longer for any of these healing activities to take effect. Be patient with yourself and your body and continue to work with your doctor or other medical professionals to manage your symptoms while you are engaging in these healing activities.

Measuring Vagus Nerve Function

It can sometimes feel like every major illness you can think of is caused by vagus nerve dysfunction. But the vagus nerve is not the only factor in our health and wellness. Therefore, as you are being working with the vagus nerve, it's important to measure its function, so that you can determine what illness are caused by the vagus nerve, and what illness are triggered by other causes.

The first, and most common, way to measure vagus nerve function is by measuring your vagal tone. To do this, breathe in deeply, and then slowly breathe out. Count your heartbeats as you breathe in and count them again as you breathe out. You should end up with two numbers, that you can put one over the other. Your vagal tone will look something like this: 9/6. That's nine heartbeats while breathing in, and six heartbeats breathing out.

The bigger the difference between these two numbers, the better your vagal tone. So, for example, 9/4 is better than 9/6. The reason that we can use such a system is because your heart rate speeds up slightly when you breathe in and slows down when you breathe out. The more your heart can slow, the easier it is for your body to calm down after stimulation. If your body is unable to calm itself down, this is a primary indicator that the vagus nerve has been compromised and is regulating the body in a state of stress, no matter how relaxed you may feel.

This slight speeding up and slowing down of the heart with each breath is called respiratory sinus arrhythmia, or RSA. When using this method to measure vagal tone, however, there are a few things to keep in mind. Your RSA (and, by extension, your vagal tone) is higher when lying down than when sitting up. You can choose to measure your RSA either way, but if you are trying to track its improvement, make sure that you are always in the same position when taking a reading. For example, if you take your first reading lying down, when you check again, you should also make sure that you're lying down.

It's also important to note that RSA declines naturally with age, and that there is to flat acceptable rate for RSA. In other words, everyone's heart beats slightly differently. If you are using RSA to measure vagal functionality, it's best to use it as a measure of your improvement, rather than relying on it as a judgment of whether your vagus nerve is working properly. In other words, no matter where your RSA is at the beginning of the month, after four weeks of consistently working to stimulate the vagus nerve, you should notice an increase in your RSA at the end of the month.

A less exact method of measuring vagus nerve function is by measuring heart rate variability. Most of the nerves responsible for regulating the heart's pace making activity are vagus nerves, which means trouble with the heartbeat almost always indicates dysfunction of the vagus nerve. A healthy heart should beat between 60-100 times per minute. If your heartbeat is faster than this while you are sitting and resting, this could indicate dysfunction of the vagus nerve.

Believe it or not, the time between each heartbeat isn't exact. Furthermore, it shouldn't be exact. While there is such a thing as an irregular heartbeat (which can also indicate trouble with the vagus nerve), a healthy heart should have a slight variation in the time between each beat. This slight variation is called heart variability. Strange as it may sound, your heartbeat can be too regular.

Low heart variability isn't a health condition in and of itself. But it's a sign that our body is operating under a certain level of stress. When we are in danger, our heart beats faster, but it also beats with more regularity. It begins to pound at a strong, steady pace, pumping oxygenated blood to our organs and muscles as fast as possible. When we come back to a state of safety, the heart will then relax, and return to its normal, slightly offbeat rhythm. This change in pace is almost entirely regulated by the vagus nerve. Therefore, low heart variability almost certainly indicates trouble with the vagus nerve.

There are other ways to measure vagal tone, but they aren't as easy to do at home. For example, the heart makes a sound when it beats. Measuring the frequency of your heartbeat is also a reliable indicator of vagal tone (sometimes called vagal sound when measured in this way). A healthy heart should measure between 0.15 and 0.4 Hz. Anything else indicates trouble with the heart, and specifically with its pace making activity. This, in turn, implicates trouble with the vagus nerve as well.

Vagal tone is being measured by an increasing number of healthcare professionals, especially in young children. It may not surprise you to learn that people with low vagal tone are typically at a much higher risk for psychological issues like emotional regulation, anxiety, internalizing disorders, and externalizing disorders. However, as the relationship between brain and body becomes more apparent, the link between vagal tone and physical health problems is steadily becoming clearer. Vagal tone is increasingly being measured in children diagnosed with autism. Children with high vagal tone also tend to exhibit more empathetic responsiveness and less social inhibition than children with low vagal tone.

Basic Exercises to Activate the Vagus Nerve

Find the exercises that work for you! All of them work, and all of them work well. For optimum stimulation of the vagus nerve, do at least two minutes of breathing exercises and ten minutes of physical exercise every day.

Breathing Exercises

Valsalva Maneuver

Take a deep breath in. Now close your mouth, pinch your nose, and gently breathe out. Hold this for a moment, and then release your nose to let out your breath. This technique will create a gentle pressure in the chest cavity, which, in turn, stimulates the vagus nerves connected to the lungs and airways.

Diaphragmatic Breathing

The diaphragm is a bell-shaped muscle located directly beneath the lungs. When you inhale, the muscle flattens out, acting as a kind of pump to allow the lungs to expand. When you breathe from the diaphragm, you breathe deeply to fill the chest. You'll notice your stomach expands outward, and contracts when you exhale.

There are two basic ways to breathe from the diaphragm. The first is to simply breathe! Sit in a quiet place with your back straight. Sit either in a cross-legged position, or with the feet planted firmly on the floor. Take a deep breath, making a conscious effort to fill the chest with air. Hold it for a moment, and then breathe out. Do this for at least two minutes. The other way is to sing! For your lungs to get enough air to sing, you must breathe from the diaphragm. So, when you start to sing, you automatically breathe from the diaphragm. Otherwise, you wouldn't have enough air to push through your vocal cords and no sound would come out. Put on a song you like and sing along. If you do this every day, you're giving your diaphragm a good workout and you're giving your vagus nerve both psychological and physical stimulation.

Audible Breathing

Normally your breath is silent. When your exhale is audible, however, it means that the glottis is partially closed. The glottis is located at the back of your tongue. The vagus nerve is connected to the glottis and stimulating this part of the tongue stimulates the vagus nerve.

For audible breathing exercises, find a quiet place to sit with your back straight. Sit in a cross-legged position or sit with your feet planted firmly on the floor. Take a deep breath and hold it for a moment. When you exhale, sigh or hiss out your breath. Think of the sound you made as a child to breathe on a cold window in order to fog it up. Breathe in this way for at least two minutes.

7-11 Diaphragmatic Breathing Exercise (Turner, 2019)

Find a quiet place to sit with your back straight. Sit with your legs crossed or your feet planted firmly on the floor. Inhale through your nose, filling the chest cavity with air, and count to seven. Hold your breath for one second, then exhale audibly through the mouth, making a sigh or a hissing sound. Exhale for a count of 11. This is one cycle. Repeat this for six-12 cycles a day.

Obstructed Diaphragmatic Breathing Exercise

Find a quiet place to sit with your back straight. Sit with your legs crossed or your feet planted firmly on the floor. Inhale through your nose, filling the chest cavity with air, until you can't take in even one more drop of air. Then purse your lips and exhale forcefully, almost as if you are blowing all the air out of your lungs. Do this until you can't exhale any more. This is one cycle. Repeat this for 6-12 cycles a day.

Physical Exercises

Walking

Going for a walk 30-60 minutes a day is a very easy way to stimulate the vagus nerve. It's not just the physical activity that makes this exercise so effective. Exposure to sunlight and fresh air also stimulate the brain and sensory nerves. Walking stimulates the heart and blood vessels and breathing in the fresh air stimulates and lungs and airways. If you are walking at a quick pace, 30 minutes will do. If you want to go slow and take your time, it's better to go for about an hour. If it's cold outside, dress warmly and walk anyway. Cold air on the face has been found to stimulate the vagus nerve, though it's still unclear why. It may have something to do with the connection between the nerve and the facial muscles. Either way, a brisk winter wind and cold air in the lungs is a great stimulating supplement to the cardiovascular activity of walking.

High-Intensity Interval Sprinting

High-intensity interval sprinting stimulates the vagus nerve by waking up the heart and lungs. Doing these one to two times a week will provide the necessary stimulation to the nerve.

To do this exercise, run as fast as you possibly can for 30 seconds, and then walk for two minutes. This is one cycle. Repeat this cycle for just 10 minutes to get a full workout.

Cardio Machines

Treadmills or other walking machines at the gym are great if you don't have a good place to walk outdoors. Especially for those who live in cold climates, taking advantage of a treadmill at the gym or even investing in one for the home is a good way to keep you walking every day, indoors or out.

Jump Rope

Did you ever jump or skip rope as a child? Believe it or not, this childhood game is a great way to get your heart beating and your lungs expanding with fresh air. Find a simple child's jump rope and jump for two to five minutes a day to stimulate the vagus nerve. This can be done indoors (of course), but if you can, try to do it outside to get the extra benefits of fresh air and sun exposure.

Inflammation, and Diseases Associated with Vagus Nerve

Nearly every autoimmune disease is caused by inflammation in the body. In fact, a great number of diseases, in general, are due to inflammation in the tissues. It is a big problem and one that pills can't really fix, though anti-inflammatories will lower it somewhat.

Inflammation has been linked to some of the deadliest diseases today, including diabetes, cancer, stroke, heart disease, and others. It has also been connected to autism and mental health issues, as well as several other brain diseases. Inflammation can kill you, but it's not entirely bad.

A study done by Dr. Harold A. Silverman at the Laboratory for Biomedical Science at the Feinstein Institute for Medical Research showed some interesting connections between inflammation and the vagus nerve. It showed that if the vagus nerve has a low tone, then the body is at higher risk for increased and chronic inflammation. This prolonged inflammation could cause issues like rheumatoid arthritis and other conditions associated with long term inflammation in the body.

What Is Inflammation?

Before we look further at how the vagus nerve influences inflammation, you should understand what inflammation all is about. It's an essential part of the immune system, so in small doses, it is something you want to happen in the body, to a certain point. Sometimes it seems to overload, and that's when it becomes too much to handle.

Inflammation is when the tissues swell and redden. They may become hot to the touch, as well. It is the natural immune response to something irritating. For example, if you get a splinter in your skin, it is viewed as a foreign object and an irritant. Your immune system responds by inflaming the idea to help the body expel and rid itself of the irritant.

However, irritants aren't just actual foreign bodies. They can be germs, bacteria, viruses, or even medications or treatments for other diseases, like chemicals, chemotherapy, or radiation. Specific areas of inflammation have names, usually ending in "itis" such as dermatitis, which is inflammation of the skin, or bronchitis, which is an inflammation of the bronchi. Symptoms get worse as the inflammation gets worse. It will start out with heat, swelling, pain, and redness, moving on to loss of function of the area that is affected. An inflamed joint will become impossible to move, and inflamed bronchi will make it tough to breathe.

As the inflammation worsens, you will start to feel sick and tired. A fever may occur, as well, another sign that your immune system is working overtime to eliminate the disease that has invaded. Your body will pour all energy into fighting the bacteria or virus, and the fever raises your metabolism, making it possible for the body to produce more antibodies and white blood cells.

Blood vessels tend to dilate to allow more blood flow to the affected area, which is necessary to get the white blood cells to the area of inflammation. This also causes a lot of pain, which is another protective mechanism. You will tend not to move a body part that is hurting, and you'll keep it protected.

The swelling that becomes evident at the site of infection is due to more and more fluid and blood cells rushing to the area. Once the irritant has been dealt with, the fluid level drops, and the swelling goes down. You will notice this, particularly in the nose when you have a cold or flu. The extra fluid helps eliminate the viruses, but it makes it hard to breathe through your nose when it is all swollen inside, thanks to inflammation of the mucous membranes.

When there is an actual threat to the body, this immune system response is invaluable and could even save your life. Unfortunately, inflammation isn't always helpful, and if it occurs outside an actual threat, it can cause a lot of issues. In fact, it is the main reason we have an autoimmune disease, which is when the body's immune system mistakes its own cells for an intruder and fights against it.

While it started out as a part of a healthy, functioning body, inflammation has become rampant in our lives for a variety of reasons. The SAD (standard American diet) that so many enjoy triggers inflammation throughout the body. Things like sugar, processed grains, and food additives can all contribute to this. In addition, people use more medications than ever before. As I've mentioned, this was my personal trigger for vagus nerve damage, but it all starts with inflammation.

The problem here is that inflammation and chronic sickness create a terrible cycle. The illness creates inflammation, and the inflammation worsens the illness. Add in all the other factors in life that are contributing to the inflammation of everything, and you have a serious problem that is very difficult to fix.

How Much Inflammation is Too Much?

Since inflammation is obviously a very important part of the immune system, you don't want to eradicate it completely. When do you know that it's too much? That's the big question that everyone wants to know the answer to.

If you are sick, some inflammation is normal. For example, when your nasal membranes swell up as you have a cold, it's a normal part of fighting off the virus. This isn't overkilling, and it will help your body recover faster. The same goes for when you are injured. A scraped knee will tend to get red and swollen for a day or two, then it subsides. If your immune system is doing its job properly, you don't have to worry.

The problem starts when things get out of hand. If you're not sick or injured, but you are experiencing inflammatory responses, something may be wrong. When multiple body parts become inflamed for apparently no reason, it can also be an indication that the immune system is malfunctioning. Where it may be normal for one knee to swell up due to an injury, even one you don't recall happening, it's not normal for your shoulders, knees, and wrists to swell, heat up, and get red. This would probably indicate an overload of inflammatory hormones.

Another indication that it may be too much inflammation is when it lasts longer than the average disease. Inflammatory symptoms that continue far beyond the usual 3-7 days for a virus or several days or weeks past what would be normal for an injury can indicate a poorly functioning immune system.

Your doctor can help you diagnose an inflammatory issue since it will also tend to show up in blood tests. However, your own experiences can also tell you if you have a problem. You know your body best and will be able to determine if there is something going on with it.

Autoimmune Diseases Caused by Inflammation

Once the body starts fighting its own cells, a war begins in you. This can be horribly uncomfortable, but it gets worse. When your immune system is busy fighting off an imaginary threat, it is more susceptible to other diseases sneaking in. You may find that if you suffer from an autoimmune disease, you also deal with a lot of colds and flu. You may feel like you catch every bug going by, and that's because you do. When the immune system is fighting this hard, it can't stop everything, and germs will get past the lowered protective barriers.

Autoimmune diseases are varied in how they present, but they all have one thing in common . . . the immune system is fighting against your own body. Here are some of the more common diseases associated with this issue.

Addison's disease: The adrenal glands are the affected organs in this disease. They produce several hormones, including androgen, aldosterone, and cortisol. Without these, the body can become quite imbalanced. You'll tend to lose weight, feel weak and exhausted, and your blood sugar will usually below. This also causes excess potassium to wind up in the blood, while sodium levels drop drastically.

Autoimmune vasculitis: When the immune system attacks blood vessels, it can cause serious issues. The resulting inflammation squeezes the arteries and veins, nearly closing them and preventing proper circulation. This causes some pretty obvious health risks that should be avoided.

Celiac disease: Also referred to as gluten sensitivity, this is an autoimmune disease where gluten causes the immune system to attack the small intestine when passing through. This results in inflammation and can cause leaky gut. It's a very serious disease, and even a small amount of gluten can trigger an immune response.

Grave's disease: This autoimmune disease causes the thyroid to overproduce hormones. Too many thyroid hormones will speed up your metabolism and can speed up your heart rate, cause extreme weight loss, anxiety, and heat intolerance. One of the most notable and unpleasant symptoms of Grave's disease is eyes that bulge out of the head.

Hashimoto's: You may have heard of this disease, which also affects the thyroid. However, unlike Grave's, Hashimoto's causes the thyroid to stop functioning properly, and it has the opposite effect on the body, causing weight gain. You'll tend to be sensitive to cold, and your hair will fall out. It can also cause goiters, or the swelling of the thyroid to the point that it forms a large lump on the neck.

Inflammatory bowel disease: Commonly known as IBD, there are a few sub-diseases under this. It refers to inflammation of the intestinal walls, but depending on where it is, the disease has a specific name.

Crohn's disease affects any part of the digestive tract, even outside the intestines. It can cause inflammation from anus to mouth, though it generally only affects a certain section of the GI tract. Ulcerative colitis is specifically limited to the colon and rectum and is caused by massive inflammation there.

Lupus: Systemic lupus erythematosus is another autoimmune disease that you have probably heard of. Originally thought to be a skin issue, it has now become evident that lupus affects many internal organs as well. Most commonly, the immune system attacks the brain, kidneys, joints, and the heart, causing pain and fatigue.

Multiple sclerosis: MS is one of the more deadly autoimmune diseases. In this case, the nervous system is attacked, and the protective myelin around the nerves is destroyed. This results in poor communication between the body and brain, which makes people feel numb and gradually lose the ability to walk and balance. It slowly robs the affected person of their ability to move and do things on their own, even affecting speech, until eventually, it affects even heart and lung function.

Psoriasis: Everyone grows new skin cells on a regular basis, and we are constantly losing or shedding old skin cells. With psoriasis, the immune system attacks the skin and causes the cells to grow far too fast. They build up in patches and become inflamed and itchy. Psoriasis can also pass to the joints and cause a form of arthritis that is very painful.

Rheumatoid arthritis: This form of autoimmune disease involves the joints. Your immune system goes after the joints, and you'll find that your joints tend to be hot, red, and stiff. It can be so painful as to affect your daily activities.

Sjögren's syndrome: In this syndrome, the glands that keep your mouth and eyes lubricated are affected. It can also attack the joints, causing inflammation there, but the most common symptoms are dry eyes and mouth.

Type 1 diabetes mellitus: Your pancreas is responsible for secreting insulin to regulate the blood sugar levels throughout the body. However, with this type of diabetes, your immune system fights against the pancreas. This destroys the cells that are responsible for making insulin and causes the patient to take insulin via injection for life.

These are just a few of the many autoimmune diseases that can affect you. They tend not to be constant but can have what is referred to as flares, where the symptoms become much worse for a period. This often coincides with high stress, sickness, or other issues that place more pressure on the body.

Signs that you have an inflammation problem, or an autoimmune disease include:

-Aches and pains
-Swelling
-Redness in specific areas
-Low-grade fever
-Fatigue

- Hair falling out
- Rashes on skin
- Tingling in the extremities
- Difficulty focusing
- Memory issues

If these symptoms persist, even after you should be over a regular cold or other illness, it's possible your immune system is attacking your body itself. The resulting inflammation could become worse and then improve, but it will likely continue to be an issue until the underlying problem is resolved.

While immune system responses that because disease are becoming more common now, it may be brought under control by using vagus nerve stimulation, which reduces inflammation.

Managing Inflammation with Vagus Nerve Stimulation

Inflammation is controlled by the vagus nerve, and when it is low in tone, you will find that there is a lot more inflammation in your body. When the nerve is stimulated, it lets the immune system know that it should calm down. The result is less chronic inflammation and better health.

Your immune system can malfunction just like everything else in the body, but when it does, it has widespread effects. Chronic inflammation will cause poor health and can even result in death if it gets bad enough. That's right, and your own body can kill you if the inflammation gets out of control. Therefore, people die from autoimmune diseases.

It's obviously best to prevent mistaken immune system responses, but the current method is to dose people up with medications that lower the immune system. These are the same drugs used to treat cancer, and they have their own side effects. It's also not a good idea to restrict your immune system for long periods of time, as this can leave you open to a lot of other diseases and will limit your lifestyle.

It's far better to aim for natural methods of reducing inflammation. Eating a healthy diet and eliminating sugar and processed foods from your diet is a good start, but frequent stimulation of the vagus nerve is also useful. It will help your body lower the inflammation and prevent the creation of more white blood cells, which can be an issue when there are too many of them.

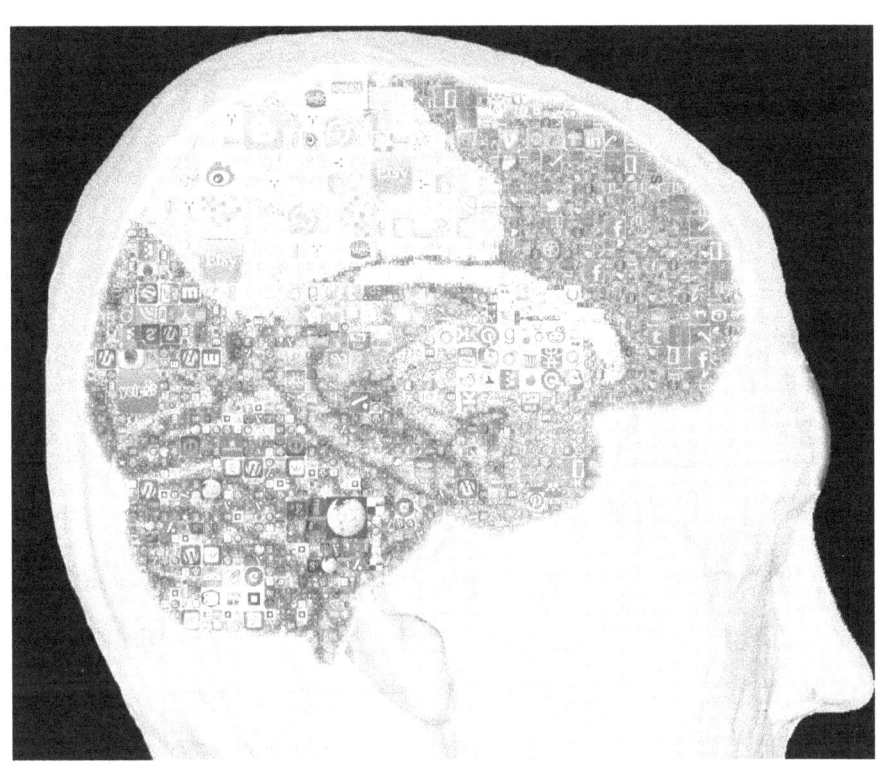

The Benefits of Vagus Nerve Stimulation

The thought of going to the hospital or seeking some form of treatment usually feels us with dread. They are synonymous with pain and suffering, and while no one likes going to the doctor, we all get infections or ailments from time to time that requires medical care and treatment. However, there are ways that we can tap into the natural self-healing power of the body and reduce the number of times that we need to seek medical intervention,

Diseases are a natural part of life because our bodies are susceptible to the wear and tear that comes with age as well as infections and physical damage inflicted by pathogens and other stimuli. This means that the quest for good health is a never-ending journey because we cannot escape the inevitable effect of nature and our surroundings on our health.

Whether you find your comfort at the bottom of the pill bottle, or in alternative therapies, our goal ultimately remains the same; to improve our quality of life by staying healthy and avoiding diseases. The quest for longevity has led to the development of research in various aspects of medicine, from disease prevention, diagnosis, treatment, and cure, the winding road to better health has led to important findings that we can use to better our health.

While human advances in medicine cannot be downplayed, it is important to remember that medicine has side effects on the body. When taken for prolonged periods of time, conventional medicine can have adverse effects on our bodies in the form of side effects. While conventional medicine is beneficial for the treatment of various ailments and conditions, we should do the necessary to reduce the incidences where we need to take it and avoid over-reliance on pills and potions.

In an ideal situation, being able to stimulate the vagus nerve effectively will enable the body to become more adept at keeping illnesses at bay, meaning that you will need less medical intervention to stay healthy. The body's self-healing mechanism functions best when the internal environment is in a rested state.

This means that when the fight and flight responses are activated, the body's self-healing mechanism cannot work. Therefore, when you unleash the parasympathetic power of the vagus nerve through stimulation, you effectively shut down the fight or flight responses and activate the body's self-healing mechanisms.

The 10th cranial nerve, which is the Vagus nerve, is the longest nerve in the body extending from the brain through the neck and thorax all the way to the gut. This nerve, with its sensory and motor response functions, has significant roles in the regulation of organs such as the heart, lungs, and gut. The parasympathetic roles of the vagus nerve, which inhibit the effects of the sympathetic nervous system, meaning that the vagus nerve is an important factor for proper organ function and optimum physical and mental health.

The roles of the vagus nerve in maintaining homeostasis and balance in the internal environment of the body have led to the discovery that the vagus nerve can be used not only in boosting our overall immunity but also in facilitating the body's self-healing mechanism.

Now that we can appreciate how important the vagus nerve is when it comes to good health, the next question would be, how do you measure the activity of the vagus nerve? That is where the vagal tone comes in.

Vagal Tone

Vagal tone is the term used to refer to the activity of the vagus nerve. The activity of the vagus nerve has significant effects on:

- heart rate regulation
- vasodilation and constriction of vessels,
- glandular activity in the heart,
- glandular activity lungs
- gastrointestinal sensitivity and motility and
- regulation of inflammation.

When it comes to health, the vagal tone is measured in terms of the consistent nature of the parasympathetic action that the vagus nerve exerts. While the vagal input is constant, the degree of the stimulation it exerts is influenced by various factors including the parasympathetic responses of the autonomic nervous system. This means that the vagal tone will vary depending on the internal environment in the body. For instance, when the body is in a state of fight or flight, then the vagal tone or activity will be diminished.

Vagal tone can be used as an indicator of various organ functions in the body, including cardiac function, and may also be used in assessing emotional regulation or any other factors that can be influenced by parasympathetic responses such as digestive functions.

The measurement of vagal tone is done using either invasive or noninvasive procedures. Measurement of the vagal tone using invasive procedures is characterized by the use of manual or electrical methods to stimulate the vagus nerve. When it comes to non-invasive techniques, the vagal tone is typically determined by the assessment of the heart rate and heart rate variability. Heart rate variability (HRV) is the difference in the time lapse that occurs between heartbeats.

When the vagal tone is high, then the heart rate is typically slower, and on the other hand, an increased heart rate is an indication that vagus nerve activity is diminished. The vagal tone in the body is a useful tool in the determination of emotional, psychological, and even possible physical disorders that may manifest as a result of poor vagal activity or function.

Vagus Nerve Stimulation

The vagus nerve has both afferent and efferent functions in connecting the brains to organs such as the heart, lungs, and gut. This means that it facilitates communication from the brain to the organs (afferent) and communication to the brain from the organs (efferent).

The vagus nerve functions in controlling motor responses in the voice box, diaphragm, heart, and stomach. In addition, it has sensory functions in the ears and tongue. The widespread nature of the influence on the vagus nerve on different organs, therefore, makes it a useful treatment therapy in patients with diseases caused by chronic inflammation, including Alzheimer's, Epilepsy, and Rheumatoid arthritis.

When Vagus nerve stimulation therapy is to be used on a patient, a device that is similar to a pacemaker is implanted in the chest of the patient. A wire from this device is then run from the device to the vagus nerve in the neck by making incisions on the left side of the neck, which allows for the wire to be placed beneath the skin. This device then functions by sending electrical impulses to the vagus nerve which, in turn, transmits these signals to the brain.

These pulses that are transmitted to the brain are used in the treatment of patients with conditions such as drug-resistant depression. The impulses help in battling depression by affecting the circuits in the limbic system of the brain, which is the area that is responsible for our moods and emotions.

In epilepsy, vagus nerve stimulation therapy works in a similar manner. The signals transmitted from the implanted device travel to the vagus nerve, where they are then sent on to the brain. These mild electrical pulses sent to the brain help in controlling the abnormal brain activity that causes epileptic seizures. While vagus nerve stimulation therapy does not cure epilepsy, it plays a big role in reducing the frequency, duration, and severity of epileptic seizures. This therapy has become an important tool in the management of epilepsy.

Perhaps one of the most incapacitating illness, that is caused by chronic inflammation in the joints is rheumatoid arthritis. Not only does it result in severe joint pain, but rheumatoid arthritis also restricts movement as well, and may lead to joint deformities in the long run. This disease is challenging for patients because it severely affects the quality of life by limiting the independence of the sufferer. It has no cure meaning that the patient needs to learn to limit and slow down the degeneration in the joints.

Vagus nerve stimulation therapy has proven to be useful in the management of the inflammation that causes joint degradation, and as such, helping in slowing down the course of rheumatoid arthritis and minimizing symptoms such as joint pain and swelling. When the vagus nerve is activated, it releases acetylcholine and inhibits the production of the tumor necrosis factor from the pancreas.

Both of these mechanisms initiated by the vagus nerve are effective in the reduction of inflammation, and therefore, offer relief in terms of the level of inflammation in terms of swelling, pain, and deformation of the joints. In rheumatoid arthritis, vagus nerve stimulation therapy can be invasive, as in the case of surgically implanting a device to function as a pacemaker or non-invasive where the vagus nerve is stimulated externally.

Vagus nerve stimulation therapy has been used in the treatment of patients with gastroparesis.

Gastroparesis is the condition where food movement through the gut is inhibited, resulting in food staying in the stomach too long and blockages being formed. This disease can lead to bacterial infections, abdominal pain, bloating, loss of appetite, and weight loss. Vagus nerve therapy functions by innervating the muscles in the digestive tract that facilitate the movement of food in the digestive system through peristalsis.

These are all classic examples of situations where vagus nerve therapy is used in conjunction with conventional medical intervention to realize quicker treatment or aid in alleviating symptoms that do not necessarily respond to medical pills. However, vagus nerve activation is not only useful for people who are already sick. This nerve can help you in maintaining and improving your physical health and mental state, and as such, we can all benefit from the self-healing powers of this powerful nerve that makes up part of the body's self-healing mechanism.

Cardiovascular Health

The vagus nerve functions in the control of our heart rate, in effect, acting as a natural pacemaker. By stimulating heart muscles, it can effectively slow down our heart rate when it is too fast as happens in stressful conditions. When the heart rate is increased, it can lead to elevation of the blood pressure, which causes strain on the heart tissue and blood vessels. By lowering the heart rate, the vagus nerve effectively reduces blood pressure, and by extension, reduces the pressure on the cardiac muscles. A properly functioning vagus nerve is, therefore, crucial for cardiovascular health and in avoiding conditions such as hypertension.

Prevention Of Inflammation

When out tissues get infected, the body responds to the attack by activating the immune system, which dispatches white blood cells to the scene of infection to neutralize the threat. These responses result in inflammation, which is characteristic in cases of physical injury or illness.

However, when an inflammatory response triggered by the immune system is prolonged, it causes the body to start attacking its own cells resulting in chronic inflammation. Chronic inflammation leads to autoimmune conditions such as rheumatoid arthritis. The vagus nerve is able to effectively control inflammation by inhibiting the overstimulation of the immune system that is caused by the sympathetic nervous system. Medical research has shown that stimulation of the vagus nerve helps in resolving conditions related to prolonged inflammation of tissues in the body.

Breathing

Our ability to breathe is controlled by our lungs, which are regulated by the Vagus nerve through the neurotransmitter acetylcholine. Proper breathing is not only an effective way to deal with pain but is also effective in coping with stress by creating a calming effect on the body.

Relaxation techniques such as meditation and yoga incorporate breathing techniques because proper breathing has a relaxing effect on the body.

Improved Memory

Stimulation of the vagus nerve has been found to have an effect on improving memory. This is accomplished through the neurotransmitter norepinephrine being released into the amygdala, which forms part of the limbic system. This means that the activation of the vagus nerve can be beneficial in counteracting the effects of some cognitive disorders.

Weight Management

Communication in the gut-brain axis is facilitated by the vagus nerve. When the vagus nerve function is impaired, it loses the sensitivity that enables it to detect fullness in the stomach. When the vagus nerve cannot send a message to the brain that the stomach is full, it means you will not be able to know when you are full or not, and this is likely to cause overeating. Stimulating the vagus nerve increases its sensitivity to the fullness signal from the stomach, and this increased sensitivity will cause you to feel fuller faster and, as such, will result in reduced food intake.

Stress Management

When the body's sympathetic responses have been activated, we go into flight and fight mode. One of the characteristics of being in fight or flight mode is the release of the stress hormone cortisol. Cortisol is a stress hormone released by the adrenal glands. The sympathetic system triggers the release of cortisol in response to various stress factors.

However, when cortisol levels remain elevated for prolonged periods of time, it has a myriad of harmful effects, including weight gain, high blood pressure, insomnia, and chronic fatigue. The vagus nerve, with its parasympathetic effects of inhibiting sympathetic responses, can effectively inhibit the release of cortisol by putting your body back into a rested and relaxed state. It is for this reason that people with a stronger vagus nerve response recover faster from illness or stress.

Gut Feelings

Have you ever been walking on a dark street and felt the hairs on the back of your neck stand up? Or just met a person and had an instinctive response that you could not really explain? Well, that is called a gut feeling, and though many of us regard them as fancies or whims, gut feelings are actually very real. The gut is capable of conveying your feelings to the brain through the vagus nerve in the form of electrical impulses. This communication facilitated by the vagus nerve through the gut-brain axis is vital to our mental health as it impacts how we behave.

Understanding PTSD, Trauma

Trauma is something everyone experiences at some point in their lives. While it can be overcome, trauma can have a long-lasting impact on an individual, causing distress diminishing self-worth, and causing a wide range of psychological concerns. On top of the psychological effects, trauma can greatly impair an individual's physical health due to its side effects.

What Is Trauma?

Trauma occurs as a natural response from the body trying to cope and manage overwhelming, disturbing, and stressful situations or events. Trauma can cause an individual to feel hopeless, depressed, and significant distrust. Traumatic events can occur for multiple reasons such as:

- Natural disasters
- War
- Loss of control over oneself
- Betrayal
- Abuse (physical, verbal, or emotional)
- Events that cause an individual to question their abilities
- Accidents
- Medical conditions
- Physical pain
- Personal assault or non-personal assault.

Types Of Trauma

Trauma is often classified under two categories, small t traumas, and large T traumas. The trauma an individual experience is solely based on the way they perceived the situation and the effect it has on them. The two categories of trauma are simply set up as a guideline to determine the level of trauma one has experienced.

Small "t" Trauma

These types of trauma do not comprise of physical threats to the individual and their life is typically not in imminent danger. Small "t" traumas are often disregarded are rarely addressed. They can include:

- Financial strain

- Work stress

- Starting a new job

- Relationship conflicts

- Legal troubles.

Many life changes can fall into the small "t" trauma category. When unaddressed, however, these types of trauma can follow an individual for their lifetime and unknowing cause additional issues. When trauma is left unprocessed or ignored, these small "t" traumas can cause a build-up of anxiety and stress. Most of these traumas are usually easy to overcome and move on from.

Large "T" Trauma

These types of trauma are more challenging to deal with and they bring about an insurmountable amount of distress and feelings of helplessness. Many times, these events will only occur once in a lifetime; others can be prolonged events that lead an individual seeing no end of the distress in sight. Large "T" trauma is not easily ignored but many individuals try to avoid them at all costs. Types of large "T" trauma can include:

- Emotional abuse

- Verbal abuse

- Physical abuse

- Sexual abuse

- Child abuse

- Neglect
- Natural disasters.

Large "T" traumas can carry several triggers that remind the individual of the event. While people who experience this try to avoid thinking about these triggers. Avoidance typically leads to more severe reactions. For an individual to fully move on from a large "T" trauma, they need to first properly heal from the pain and distress it has caused. While this is not easily or quickly accomplished, it is necessary for them to return to a more normal way of life.

Acute Stress Disorder

Mild trauma can lead to acute stress disorder. This can cause a person to have a variety of traumatic symptoms, but they tend to only last for a few weeks and can slowly go away on their own.

Trauma can cause mental, physical, and psychological symptoms, which can include:

- Sadness
- Fear
- Shame
- Anger
- Nausea
- Dizziness

- Sleep disturbances
- Headaches
- Digestive issues
- Loss of appetite
- Insomnia
- Irregular emotional control
- Anxiety
- Addiction
- Depression.

When trauma is left untreated or not appropriately processed, these conditions can worsen and become debilitating. The side effect can lead to more severe health problems.

What Is Ptsd?

PTSD can arise out of traumatic occurrences. Those with PTSD tend to have symptoms of trauma and/or acute stress disorder but the symptoms never diminish and can last for months or longer. The longer the symptoms are present, the more debilitating and severe they become. This type of trauma is often the result of a person being directly or indirectly affected by a physical attack. The traumatic events cause the individual to ruminate over the experience. Disturbing thoughts, feelings, and flashbacks haunt the individual and these can remain present for months and years after the traumatic event has happened.

Those with PTSD have a negative reaction to anything that reminds them of the trauma. They can act out aggressively and abusively exhibit behavior that can be viewed as detached or erratic. The symptoms tend to be grouped into four categories, but the severity of the symptoms can range greatly. These symptom categories include:

    1. Intrusive thoughts

These symptoms include memories, dreams, and flashbacks that occur involuntarily. Each of these can be incredibly realistic to the individual suffering from PTSD that they can often mistake their flashbacks or daydreams as actually occurring in real time. These symptoms affect the individual significantly as they cause the person to unwilling relive the event repeatedly.

    2. Avoidance

When individuals face such intense traumatic events, it is not uncommon for them to want to avoid talking or thinking about the events. Those with PTSD go out of their way to avoid remembering any details about the event. They will often make a point to avoid people, places, situations, objects, or activities that can remind them of what they experienced. This avoidance carries over to avoiding how they feel about the events.

    3. Negative thoughts or feelings

Negative thoughts of those with PTSD go far beyond the usual negative self-talk that most participate in. Those with PTSD have a constant loop of negativity whirling in their heads, both about how they feel about themselves and about those around them. PTSD can cause a person to lose trust in their closest friends and family and they may even feel these individuals may cause them harm or are out to get them. This causes individuals to immediately lose interest in the things they used to enjoy doing. They are often overcome with feelings of shame, guilt, fear, and rage and that makes it impossible for them to participate in activities they once enjoyed.

4. Reaction symptoms

Reaction symptoms are those the individual exhibit when reminded of the traumatic event. These symptoms can cause an individual to become reckless, self-destructive, easily irritated to the point that they verbally or physically lash out at things around them, unable to sleep or concentrate, and may find ways to "self-medicate" such as drinking excessively.

How Does This Impact Daily Life?

The symptoms, no matter how mild, can have significant impairments on an individual's life. When individuals hold on to past events, this has a direct impact on the autonomic nervous system. These traumas affect how we speak, how we move, how we express ourselves, and how we hold ourselves or our posture. Individuals who suffer from PTSD live impaired lives and often lack the mental, physical, and emotional capacity to function day-to-day.

PTSD can cause the manifestation of:

- Intense pain

- Digestive issues

- Hormonal imbalance

- Disruption to the immune system

- Depression

- Addiction.

How Does the Vagus Nerve Impact Trauma?

When individuals are faced with constant trauma, they are unable to allow the parasympathetic nervous system to become active and the vagus nerve reduces the fight or flight response. They often enter a state of constant shutdown where they feel they are not living their own life. This leads to confusion and the inability to recognize a safe situation, places, or people. Those who suffer from PTSD can suffer more severely from this as they are more likely to replay the traumatic events repeating through their minds. When they continuously loop these memories, it makes it more difficult for them to distinguish between what is real and what is just a recollection of past events. For individuals to learn to cope with their trauma, they need to be able to break this negative loop.

Breathing plays a major part in overcoming trauma. Those with PTSD frequently suffer from panic or anxiety attacks. This causes their breathing to be rapid and focused in the upper chest. Breathing in this manner is linked to the sympathetic nervous system and can trigger the shutdown response. This type of response to fear and trauma is associated with primitive survival skills. When you see an animal face a predator, they will often freeze and/or play dead. This is a defense mechanism they have developed to get predators to walk by instead having them for lunch. While this is effective for in the wild when facing down a lion, for humans this response is a hindrance and not the way many want to live out their days. Being able to notice and regain control over your breathing can help the vagus nerve and parasympathetic system click on. Unfortunately, this is easier said than done for those who must face the traumatic memories.

While it can take a great deal of practice being able to put a sudden stop to the shutdown response, gaining control of your breathing and working through your trauma instead of avoiding it can be done. With vagus nerve stimulation and toning, individuals can retrain their systems to react in a more appropriate manner when facing trauma. Even those with severe PTSD can benefit from learning how to perform quick vagus nerve activation techniques to help work through traumatic episodes. Through vagus nerve stimulation, those suffering through trauma and/or PTSD can rewire their process and become unstuck from the fight or flight, or shutdown, phases.

Vagus Nerve Exercises That Can Help Individuals Overcome Ptsd And Trauma

The methods described here can be used at any time, any place. Some of these allow you to quickly stimulate the vagus nerve in order to better manage your stress and anxiety. Others will need to regularly practice this in order to obtain the most benefits. Those with PTSD should consider adding these techniques and methods with additional talk and/or cognitive therapy. When used with traditional forms of therapy, one can fully learn how to address, process, and heal from their trauma.

Ways to Quickly Snap Out of the Shutdown Response Through Vagus Nerve Activation

There are three main ways in which a person can quickly snap out of the shutdown response and activate their vagus nerve:

1. Splash cold water on your face to slow the heart rate and lower the body pressure.

2. Take in a deep breath, hold it for a few seconds, and then slowly exhale through the nose; repeat three to five times.

3. Chant a simple positive mantra such as "I am safe" or "I am strong."

Vagus Nerve Stimulation to Heal from PTSD

Stimulating the vagus to stop the sympathetic system is done when the individuals feels safe and secure. The following activities can instantly promote varying levels of these feelings.

1. Make connections with others. Though challenging to feel as if you can trust others, the best way to switch from the sympathetic nervous system to the parasympathetic nervous system is to make a connection with someone else.

2. Hug. Along with the first technique, hugging helps us feel safe and connected to others. By giving or receiving a hug, you can instantly trigger the vagus nerve.

3. Laugh. If hugging is not really your thing, you can laugh instead. Laughing can help stimulate the vagus nerve to release oxytocin. Oxytocin encourages you to make connections with others and lift your mood. Laughing, just like hugging, helps you feel

connected with others and can strengthen bonds.

4. Shake it off. One of the ways you can bounce out of the shutdown mode is to do a full body shake. Before you go into a full out shake, do a quick body scan. Are there any areas of your body that feel tense or stiff? If you find tension in your body, these are the areas you want to focus on when you wiggle and shake. Give each area your attention as you shake the tension out. When you have gone through all the areas and feel relieved, pause for a moment to take in the stillness that surrounds you and let it fill you. This is your body waking up again. This is the feeling you want to recall when facing a trauma-induced memory or episode.

Daily Long-Term Vagal Toning Technique for Trauma and PTSD

Healing from trauma or PTSD can be a life-long process. Strengthening the vagus nerve daily results in developing the skills necessary for your mind and body to bounce back from traumatic events and experiences that trigger trauma symptoms. The following daily exercises you can perform to receive long-term benefits from the vagus nerve:

1. Bhramari pranayama. The Bhramari pranayama is referred to as the humming bee breath in yoga practice. This type of breath work helps you tone the vagus nerve by stimulating it through the vocal cords. When you perform this breath, you can keep the nervous system calm and prevent it from going into fight or flight mode. To perform this type of breathwork, get into a comfortable sitting position on the floor or on your bed. Cross your legs and bring your hands to cover yours ears. Your thumbs should face down towards the ground. Take a deep breath in; as you exhale, begin to make a humming sound that vibrates through your ears. You can repeat this process as many times as you need.

2. Sleep on your right side. Trauma and PTSD have severe negative effects on sleep, and how you sleep can add to these difficulties. Sleeping on the right side of your body can stimulate the vagus nerve and lead to a more restful night's sleep. You should avoid sleeping on your back as this is often the worst position for vagus nerve stimulation.

3. Tai chi or qigong. Like yoga, tai chi and qigong are forms of slow movement exercises that stimulate and tone the vagus nerve. These practices focus on strengthening the internal systems through precise moment and breath. Sun Style tai chi is a type of tai chi the utilize smooth, flowing movements that can help individuals feel grounded. This is an important aspect for those with PTSD as they can often feel lost and unsure of where they are, which results in panic, frustration, and confusion. Doing a simple Sun Style tai chi sequence can tone the vagus nerve and be an effective way to help heal from trauma.

Vagus Nerve and Anxiety Disorder

A normal day of an individual is always filled with several activities and situations. These activities can make an individual be anxious. It is a normal phenomenon for an individual to be anxious in his life. However, there are people who develop anxiety disorders over a period. Anxiety disorders are always associated with persistent, intense and excessive for of fear and worry about the situations and activities the daily of a human being is characterized with.

These feelings of anxiety are very detrimental. They have the potential of affecting an individual's day to day life. It makes it difficult for an individual to be in control of his or her day because of anxiety. It becomes even difficult since experiencing anxiety disorders goes to making a person's life to be in danger. It is because the mind perceives normal things largely out of proportion. An individual characterized by anxiety disorder is prone to avoiding the life situations that make him or her be anxious.

History Of Anxiety Disorders

These disorders were discovered by the American Psychiatric Association in the year 1980. There was a very interesting diagnosis that used to happen before this recognition. A generic diagnosis of stress and was one which was given to people who suffered from anxiety disorders. This was because medical practitioners did not understand what entailed in anxiety disorders. In turn, very few people were able to receive effective treatment leaving most people on the loop. However, there have been several types of research that have been conducted that show how people suffer a great deal with these anxiety disorders. These suffering can be avoided if these diagnosis and treatment are done in the early stages of ailment.

There have been several awareness campaigns carried out by people over the years. However, recent years have seen a major focus by the media on the prevalence of anxiety disorders. This has made several people be aware of the general knowledge about anxiety disorders. The modern years has seen development and advancements of better and appropriate ways of treating these conditions. There are more patients from different walks of life who are getting treatment for anxiety disorders. It is because the level of stigma associated with anxiety disorders has dropped.

The early years had an intriguing thought about anxiety disorders. People associated with panic attacks and anxiety disorders as a problem faced by only women. This ideology was found to be fallacious over years of research and study from interested parties. However, it is shown by studies that men tend to be less hesitant to receive treatment. This is despite the conditions affecting both men and women. These conditions have been in existence for a very long time. It is only the recent awareness and recognition that has seen the rise in patient's numbers. Several leaders in the past have been reported to experiencing panic attacks and different forms of anxiety disorders. The form of treatments offered in the past was diverse and can be termed humorous. The forms of treatment offered very ineffective to patients. There were certain moments that the forms of treatment were very dangerous to an individual. The forms of treatment in the past involved use of balms and herbs, bloodletting with the usage of leeches, application of extremely hot temperature to a patient and bathing in extremely cold rivers and lakes. This dawn was ended by the new form of psychoanalysis. One of the greatest psychologists who spearheaded the research was known as Freud. Several people turned their ways to therapeutic solutions when faced with anxiety disorders. Several advancements have been seen over the years to the development of drugs that have proved to be very helpful to people. People with an adverse level of anxiety disorders have been prescribed these drugs for their betterment.

Types Of Anxiety Disorders

1. Panic Disorder

There are moments an individual experiences panic attacks that are consistent and unexpected. The common definition of what panic attacks are is; they are surges that appear abruptly to an individual which are filled with intense levels of fears. These panic attacks can reach their peak in a couple of few seconds. People who suffer from this condition tend to leave their life in the utmost form of fear because of the panic attacks. There are several ways that an individual can know if he or she is suffering from panic attacks. A person is likely to suffer from panic attacks if he or she feels an overwhelming sense of terror which has does not have any obvious cause for it. There are also physical symptoms that characterize panic attacks. They include racing of heart, sweating and breathing complications. A large population across the globe experience panic attacks either once or twice across their lifetime. There was a recent report that was prepared by the American Psychological Association which had a critical finding. The report stated that out of seventy-five people, one person is likely to experience or ail from panic disorder. There are several things that a person who suffers from panic attack experiences. He or she can be in fear of experiencing another form of a panic attack if this situation has happened twice in a span of one month. The symptoms of panic disorders have been seen to be quite overwhelming by people. However, there is good news in the present world we live in. It is because these symptoms can be managed and be improved through the current form of treatment. An individual ailing from this condition is encouraged to seek medical help. The situation has the possibility of running a person's life because it is detrimental. It reduces a person's productivity and attainment of quality life because it affects a person's day to day life.

Symptoms of Panic Disorder

There is a certain age that the symptoms of panic disorder can manifest themselves clearly. It begins to manifest clears in teens and young adults who are around the ages of twenty-five years. An individual is termed to be suffering from panic disorders when the panic attacks happen more than four times. It was also sensible to be diagnosed with a panic disorder when you leave in constant fear and worry of experiencing panic attacks after suffering from one. There are no warning signings that are accompanied by panic attacks.

There is a period that occurs abruptly with intense levels of fear which lasts up to an estimated time of twenty to thirty minutes. There are also extreme cases of panic attacks that have been experienced by several people across the globe. This entails the problem of going to a level of panic attacks lasting up to more than one hour. Therefore, panic attacks tend to differ in the experiences of several people in the globe. The common symptoms include; shortness in breathing, increased in the heart palpitations, dizziness, sweating chest pains, fear, nausea, and lightheadedness.

2. Post-Traumatic Stress Disorder

Life events that are terrifying are the major cause of this disorder. These terrific life experiences can either have been experienced or have been witnessed by an individual. There are several things that go on when a person is suffering from posttraumatic stress. He or she is prone to having nightmares, severe anxiety and flashbacks. It goes a higher level to the person experiencing deep thoughts about the event that are uncontrollable. There are different life situations that can be traumatizing. These events include rape, terror attracts and accidents just to mention a few. They really affect an individual to the core since they affect an individual daily life. It takes time for an individual to adjust from these situations to cope with his normal lifestyle. However, this is not the endpoint for an individual suffering from post-traumatic stress. It is because; good health care can be able to make him or her get better. An individual is supposed to seek treatment from a reliable medical facility. A good form of treatment has the potential of reducing these effects that affect an individual's daily activities.

Symptoms of Post-Traumatic Stress Disorder

It has a different way its symptoms manifest themselves. They tend to manifest in an individual after an estimated time of one month. The one moth stated is after the occurrence of the traumatic event. The symptoms of posttraumatic events have a severe impact on an individual's life. They affect a person's life from his or her work and transcend to affecting his social relationships with family and friends. This leads to low productivity in the normal tasks that an individual is supposed to undertake.

This form of anxiety order symptoms is always grouped into four different groups. These groups include; negative change in thinking and moods, avoidance, changes in emotion and physical reaction, and intrusive memories. These situations are not like everybody who suffers from post-traumatic stress. This even makes the base of symptoms of posttraumatic stress being different from people who are diagnosed with the disorder.

Intrusive memories are characterized with; recurrent of stressful memories about the traumatic event, revealing of the traumatizing events as if they were reoccurring, dreams that seem upsetting and nightmares that relate to the traumatic event and severe emotional distress of anything that can remind an individual about the traumatizing experience. The symptoms categorized under avoidance include an individual avoid thinking about the traumatic event.

The category of changes in a person's mood and thoughts has several signs. Some of these symptoms include; having negative thoughts about oneself and the world in general, loss of hope about the future, having difficulty in memories, difficulty when it comes to maintaining close relationships with people, detachments from friends and family and feeling of being emotionally numb. The last category of symptoms is those that are grouped under changes in emotional and physical reactions. These symptoms include; being frightened easily, overwhelming levels of guilt, trouble when it comes to a person concentrating, trouble when it entails concentrating and development of self-destructing behavior.

3. SOCIAL ANXIETY DISORDER

It is very normal for an individual to feel a certain form of being nervous in certain situations life presents us with. A good depiction can be a person going for a date or making a huge presentation at work. These situations have the potential of making a person experience butterflies in his or her stomach. However, this is different in a person who is suffering from a social anxiety disorder which is also known as social phobia. The difference is portrayed when an individual suffering from this disorder is anxious and faced with overwhelming levels of fear and embracement from being judged and scrutinized.

The levels of fear and anxiety that individual experience in social anxiety disorder is detrimental. They have the potential of affecting an individual's daily life experiences. The life experiences cut across through educational, professional and social life. Learning to cope with the skills that psychotherapy helps to bring an individual to a recovery stage. There are cases where are an individual experience severe impact because of social anxiety disorder, an individual is prescribed drugs during these situations.

Symptoms of Social Anxiety Disorder

There are moments in life where an individual feel shy and discomfort in certain situations. These feelings sometimes are not characteristics of social anxiety disorder. People likely to have such experiences are children. The comfort a person is likely to experience largely depends on an individual's traits and his or her experiences in the present situation. Social anxiety starts to portray itself on teens. There are also moments or situations that it is seen in children and adults.

Symptoms of social anxiety disorder are characterized into two groups. These groups include behavioral and emotional symptoms and physical symptoms. Symptoms classified under behavioral and emotional signs include; fear of situations, worry about embarrassment, the fright of talking with strangers and fear of being noticed. On the other hand, symptoms related to physical symptoms include blushing, increased heart rate, sweating, muscle tension, dizziness and stomach upset.

Major Causes Of Anxiety Disorders

There are several factors that can lead to a person developing anxiety disorders. The normal life of an individual is characterized by the occurrence of different activities. These activities cut across his or her social, educational and professional edges just to mention few facets of life. These activities and situations have the potential of making an individual develop anxiety disorders over time. It is a very complicated topic for several peoples because human is different. Therefore, causes of anxiety tend to differ in several people.

The cause of anxiety can be complicated sometimes. It is because it has the potential of being caused by a combination of chained issues. These issues can either be induced by the general environment an individual is accustomed to leaving in. The common causes of anxiety from the environment an individual resides in can be life experiences, emotions or certain events. It is important for a person to know the causes of anxiety disorders. It is because it has myriad advantages such as keeping an individual in shape of his daily life to reduce or avoid the causes. These causes include:

1. Medication

Anxiety has the potential to make an individual make panic, fell restless and nervous. This happens even in a situation where an individual is not in danger. These feelings can be as a result of the medication an individual is taking because of other health conditions he or she is suffering from. There are two probable causes that these medications may bring to an individual. They have the potential of making an individual experience these attacks for the fir first time or worsen the attacks if they were experienced earlier on. These effects by drugs are normally referred to as side effects of treatments. However, there are drugs that target a specific part of a human body that plays a critical part in anxiety. They include;

a. Medications with Caffeine

There are some medications that treat migraine and headaches that have caffeine as their component. These drugs have the potential for stimulating an individual's nervous system. This has an influence on making an individual's blood pressure and heart palpitations to increase. An individual has the possibility of being jittery, anxious and nervous during these moments. An individual who is prone to anxiety attacks has the possibility of developing a disorder in moments he or she is subjected to such drugs for long.

b. Corticosteroids

These drugs have a special way in which they work in an individual 's body. They work similarly to how hormones produced in the body conduct their functions. These drugs are used to treating certain conditions in an individual's life. They are commonly used to treat bronchitis, arthritis, asthma, and allergies. These symptoms presented in anxiety disorders are presented when an individual is presented to taking cortisone, prednisone, and dexamethasone.

c. ADHD Drugs

The medications used in these cases are always described as stimulations. This means that they have a large magnitude in affecting an individual's brain. These types of drugs have the potential to change how a person's nerve cells work because they change how they send messages from the environment. The described impacts have the potential of changing how an individual's brains work. They subject a person's brain to a mental state of being anxious and restless in moments an individual takes them in high dosages. Mood swings are a common occurrence to an individual who has such prescriptions. It can lead to an anxiety disorder if these symptoms progress for a long time. The common drugs in this group include Focalin, Adderall, and Vyvanse.

d. Asthma Medications

Some of the drugs that are used to treat asthma have the potential of altering an individual's moods. This brings about mental states such as depression and anxiety to an individual's life. Medicines that are used to open an individual's brain have the potential of making him or her experience anxiety attacks. This phenomenon can occur even if an individual did not experience anxiety attacks even if he or she did not in the past. These drugs include albuterol, salmeterol, and theophylline.

e. Thyroid Medicine

There are several things that are bound to happen to an individual when his or her body does not make adequate thyroid fluid. An individual can have low levels of concentration, gain excessive weight or lack of energy to do his or her daily duties. This condition is commonly known as hypothyroidism. The drugs used to treat this condition are commonly known for making a patient experience panic attack.

f. Seizure Drugs

The type of medication used in this is commonly known as phenytoin. It is responsible for calming the electrical activities that happen in a person's brain in the event he or she experiences seizures. There are certain situations that a doctor can prescribe these drugs to a patient who has problems in his or her heartbeats to have a regular rhythm. The drug can have severe effects by triggering anxiety attacks on an individual. These drugs have the potential of making an individual become anxious and agitated.

g. Medicine Meant for Parkinson's Disease

During treatment of this condition, doctors prescribe a combination of two drugs most of the times. These drugs are carbidopa and levodopa. The release of capsules from rotary drugs can make an individual experience anxiety attack. If symptoms that are related to anxiety disorders persist on an individual, he or she is advised to have discussions with his or her doctor about a change of medication.

Body and Mind Connection

People who have great enthusiastic wellbeing know about their musings, sentiments, and practices. They have learned healthy approaches to adapt to the pressure and issues that are atypical piece of life. They like themselves and have sound connections.

In any case, numerous things that occur in your life can disturb your passionate wellbeing. These can prompt healthy sentiments of pity, stress, or tension. Indeed, even great or needed changes can be as upsetting as undesirable changes. These things include:

• Being laid off from your activity

• Having a kid leave or get back

• Dealing with the demise of a friend or family member

• Getting separated or wedded

- Suffering a disease or damage

- Getting occupation advancement

- Experiencing cash issues

- Moving to another home

- Having or embracing a child.

Your body reacts to the way you think, feel, and act. This is one sort of "mind/body connection." When you are focused on, on edge, or upset, your body responds in a way that may reveal to you that something isn't right. For instance, you may grow hypertension or a stomach ulcer after an, especially distressing occasion, for example, the passing of a friend or family member.

Way to Improved Health

There are ways that you can improve your passionate wellbeing. Initially, attempt to perceive your feelings and comprehend why you are having them. Sifting through the reasons for bitterness, stress, and uneasiness in your life can assist you with dealing with your passionate wellbeing. The following are some other supportive tips.

Discover some stunning realities about the mind-body connection:

We have the Mind-Body Connection

Regardless of whether intentionally mindful of it or not, every one of us encounters the mind-body connection regularly of our lives. Rather than thinking about the connection as something out of sight reach, or something just realistic through long stretches of yoga and reflection, recollect it is constantly here. Mouth-watering over a tasty looking sweet, or anxious "butterflies" in the stomach before making an introduction, or running a race, are overall ideal instances of characteristic personality body connections, which a large portion of us have encountered eventually. Occasionally, the mind-body connection can deliver negative results, such as neglecting to meet athletic, scholastic, or expert objectives because of dread made by the brain.

Our Bodies React to How We Think

All that we are emerges with our contemplations. With our musings, we make the world.

Buddha

As such, on the off chance that we are continually thinking negative, reckless considerations, our bodies will go with the same pattern. Enthusiastic and mental lopsidedness can begin as something like pressure incited cerebral pains, tight shoulders, and an irritated upper back, and lead to unfortunate weight increase or misfortune, a sleeping disorder, and hypertension. Then again, we can put forth a cognizant attempt to think more decidedly and to create healthy ways of dealing with stress forever's pressure and preliminaries. After some time, the condition of our passionate and psychological well-being can be harmed or help the body's resistant framework.

We Can Make Ourselves Sick & We Can Make Ourselves Well

Studies show our ways of dealing with stress and ways we handle pressure straightforwardly associate to how we manage genuine ailments, including malignant growth. Ceaseless pressure influences the body in a negative manner, and over significant stretches of time, long haul pressure can make us increasingly vulnerable to diabetes, hypertension, heart illnesses, and a few diseases.

Notwithstanding, by utilizing our intrinsic personality body connection in a constructive manner, by keeping our brains and bodies fit as a fiddle with exercise and nourishment, we can keep feelings of anxiety lower. At the end of the day, the better we can adapt by remaining quiet and decreasing mental pressure, we will thusly lessen physical worry, alongside the possibility of building up a sickness.

We Also Have a BODY-Mind Connection

If we focus, it is anything but difficult to see the effect the body has on our perspective also. For instance, when ladies' bodies are getting ready for monthly cycle, it is the hormones inside the body causing the entirety of the feared indications (cramps, swelling, weakness, enthusiastic awkwardness, and so forth.). Another case of body-mind responses is this season's cold virus. More than likely, an individual begins to feel unwell intellectually the day or a couple of days before the body uncovered the irritated throat, nasal clog, and other basic physical manifestations.

On the other side, the body-mind connection is inconceivably positive, regardless of whether it is endorphins created after exercise or stress alleviation during a back rub. In the physical stances of yoga, it is imagined that specific stances produce certain psychological states. Backbends, for instance, are thought to animate the psyche, while reversals may expedite a calmer state. Exercise can be a modest method to help our center, states of mind, and by and large wellbeing.

Nourishment Affects Both Our Bodies and Minds

It returns to that familiar adage, "We are what we eat." Every single piece or fluid going through our lips has a type of impact on our minds. Our wholesome admission, consistently, can have immense effects both negative and positive on how we feel, on account of the substance serotonin. Basically, when serotonin levels are high, we're more joyful, and when they're low, we become discouraged.

Eating such many carbs and sugar can diminish affectability to serotonin, which prompts awful states of mind, and in the long run stoutness. To adjust serotonin levels, eating protein can be the arrangement, particularly before carb admission. Rather than gobbling a sugary jolt of energy noontime, go for a nibble high in protein to keep the temperament positive and vitality up, maintaining a strategic distance from an accident later.

Standard Sleep Is a Must for Mind & Body

Besides nourishment and exercise, rest likewise assumes a tremendous job in keeping up sound serotonin levels and keeping our brains and bodies content with one another. Serotonin's essential activity in the body is to quiet, along these lines, it is intently attached to how vitality is - or isn't- used (for example exercise and rest). Without rest, our cerebrums can be contrarily influenced, by disturbing our mind's reaction to serotonin. At the end of the day, it is essential to keep up a predictable resting design, to keep the psyche and body healthy.

Reflection Can Help Our Hearts

As indicated by the American Heart Connection, medicinal proof uncovers a certifiable complementary connection between the brain and body. Practices like reflection and other unwinding strategies have appeared to change mind-body yet in addition mind-heart connections. While there is a shortage of concentrates legitimately tending to how mind-heart intercessions can help patients with the congestive cardiovascular breakdown, the AHA closed reflection could help with tension and wretchedness, which regularly match with the genuine disease.

 Pondering for around 15 minutes every day can likewise help any individual who needs to remain focused and quiet for the duration of the day. Activities like reflection can help move mental observations and responses to circumstances. By getting mindful of strain and uneasiness, and interfacing with the breath, the mind will unwind, and the body will as well. In any event, removing a couple of seconds from an upsetting day to inhale unobtrusively can have comparative impacts.

Basically, we are what we think, eat, drink, say and relax. Creating and applying care to these parts of life can assist us with maintaining blissful personality body connections. Tell us how you use your mind-body connection with remain sound.

Express your sentiments in proper manners

If sentiments of stress, trouble, or tension are causing physical issues, keeping these emotions inside can aggravate you feel. It's alright to tell your friends and family when something is annoying you. In any case, remember that your loved ones may not generally have the option to assist you with managing your emotions fittingly. On these occasions, approach somebody outside the circumstance for help. Take a stab at asking your family specialist, an instructor, or a strict consultant for guidance and backing to assist you with improving your enthusiastic wellbeing.

Carry on with a healthy lifestyle

Concentrate on the things that you are appreciative of in your life. Do whatever it takes not to fixate on the issues at work, school, or home that lead to negative sentiments. This doesn't mean you need to profess to be cheerful when you feel focused on, on edge, or upset. It's critical to manage these negative emotions, however, attempt to concentrate on the positive things throughout your life, as well. You might need to utilize a diary to monitor things that cause you to feel cheerful or serene. Some exploration has indicated that having an inspirational standpoint can improve your personal satisfaction and give your wellbeing a lift. You may likewise need to discover approaches to relinquish a few things throughout your life that cause you to feel pushed and overpowered. Set aside a few minutes for things you appreciate.

Create strength

Individuals with strength can adapt to worry in a healthy manner. Versatility can be learned and fortified with various methodologies. These incorporate having social help, keeping a positive perspective on yourself, tolerating change, and keeping things in context. An instructor or advisor can assist you with accomplishing this objective with intellectual conduct treatment (CBT). Inquire as to whether this is a smart thought for you.

Quiet your psyche and body

Unwinding techniques, for example, contemplation, tuning in to music, tuning in to guided symbolism tracks, yoga, and Tai Chi are valuable approaches to bring your feelings into balance.

Reflection is a type of guided idea. It can take numerous structures. For instance, you may do it by working out, extending, or breathing profoundly. Approach your family specialist for guidance about unwinding techniques.

Deal with yourself.

To have great passionate wellbeing, it's imperative to deal with your body by having a standard daily schedule for eating well suppers, getting enough rest, and practicing assuaging repressed pressure. Abstain from indulging and don't mishandle medications or liquor, utilizing medications or liquor worthwhile motivations different issues, for example, family and medical issues.

Interesting points

Poor passionate wellbeing can debilitate your body's insusceptible framework. This makes you bound to get colds and different diseases during genuinely troublesome occasions. Additionally, when you are feeling focused on, on edge, or upset, you may not deal with your wellbeing just as you should. You may not want to work out, eating nutritious nourishments, or taking a prescription that your primary care physician endorses. You may mishandle liquor, tobacco, or different medications. Different indications of poor passionate wellbeing include:

- Back torment

- Change in craving

- Chest torment

- Constipation or looseness of the bowels

- Dry mouth

- Extreme tiredness

- General a throbbing painfulness

- Headaches

- High pulse

- Insomnia (inconvenience dozing)

- Lightheadedness

- Palpitations (the inclination that your heart is dashing)

- Sexual issues

- Shortness of breath

- Stiff neck

- Sweating

- Upset stomach

- Weight addition or misfortune

For what reason does my primary care physician need to think about my feelings?

You may not be accustomed to conversing with your primary care physician about your sentiments or issues in your own life. In any case, recollect that the individual in question can't generally tell that you're feeling focused on, on edge, or upset just by taking a gander at you. It's imperative to be straightforward with your primary care physician on the off chance that you are having these sentiments.

In the first place, the person in question should ensure that other medical issues aren't causing your physical side effects. If your side effects aren't brought about by other medical issues, you and your PCP can address the enthusiastic reasons for your manifestations. Your primary care physician may propose approaches to treat your physical manifestations while you cooperate to improve your passionate wellbeing.

The Natural Healing Power of your Body with Self-Help Exercises and Techniques

Exercise

Exercise is a necessary part of healing from chronic pain. You don't have to become an active bodybuilder or an athlete, but some degree of body movement is highly desirable to prevent chronic pain. Body movements release the "stuck" energy in our body and ensure a smooth flow of energy to prevent any pain.

Exercising is a great way to reduce your anxiety. Whether you wake up earlier in the morning before you must go to work and go for a run, or if you can go when you get home from and jog around the block. Also, if you do exercise more this will help with your self-esteem. Exercising will make you healthier and you will feel better about yourself. If you are worried about your health and it is making your anxiety worse, get out there and do some exercises. You don't even have to leave your house; you could just find an exercise DVD and start doing some exercise from your own living room. To really help lower anxiety, it is a good idea that each time you exercise to be sure it is for 30 minutes or more. Studies have shown that it takes about thirty minutes for your anxiety to lower when exercising.

If you don't want to exercise alone, grab a friend to do this activity with you. This will make you happy and you can have someone to talk to about the things you are anxious about. It's great to have someone who you can let all your feelings be expressed to who can help you. Healthy exercise has some surprising implications for those with anxiety disorders and other psychological conditions including depression. The mechanisms by which exercise, and mental health are related are not fully understood, but many medical experts around the world now acknowledge that exercise has a major impact on a wide range of psychological conditions. It is even now believed that exercise can be as effective at combating depression as many commonly prescribed drugs.

Short bursts of activity a few times a day are the type of exercise that experts recommend. A brisk walk lasting only ten minutes is believed to be enough to raise your emotional state for a couple of hours. For those with anxiety disorders, it can be hard to get out and about on occasion. For some, with severe conditions, it can seem impossible. Exercise, however, will really help to improve your emotional state and take your mind off anxiety. Use the following tips to increase your chances of successfully incorporating exercise into your life.

Moderate level intensity exercise is recommended as perfect for improving your physical health and your mental health. This includes; walking briskly, cycling, jogging or swimming. Walking and jogging should not need any investment and if you're uncomfortable alone, partner up with a friend or relative. Ideally buddy up with someone who is addressing the same issues or has a good understanding of them, for extra support.

When we exercise, the brain releases endorphins, or "feel good" chemicals that are responsible for the "high" that many people feel during and after exercise. Another benefit of exercise for those with depression is that it lends purpose and structure to each day. Outdoor exercise has been shown to be especially effective for lifting mood.

Regular exercise can help maintain a healthy weight, which can be a problem in depressed people. Exercise promotes overall wellbeing, including heart health and a toned, more muscular body. The weight-bearing aspects of exercise prevent the body from losing bone mass and decrease the risk of osteoporosis, a particular benefit for women.

People who suffer from anxiety may not be interested in exercise. When someone is overwhelmed by the stress of everyday life, working out seems less than appealing. However, research shows that exercise plays an important role in reducing anxiety symptoms.

While exercise has been clinically proven to reduce anxiety and improve mood, it can also treat several other health problems. Health issues can be a major anxiety trigger and easing the symptoms of those ailments can reduce anxiety symptoms further.

In addition, exercising can help people relax. When a person exercises, their body releases hormones that produce a calming effect. Exercise also increases body temperature, which can be very relaxing. Working up a sweat is tiring, but it's a great way to calm down.

Speed Walking

Speed walking, more often referred to as power walking or race walking, is a technique of walking at a rapid pace. Walking is a great alternative to running and is oftentimes much easier and more accessible to a greater variety of people. Walking provides all the aerobic benefits of running while steering clear of many of the injuries associated with high-impact techniques of running. The activity of walking at an increased rate then walking "normally" can help participants lose weight, tone their muscles, and increase their mood.

Not only is speed walking valuable for the muscles and joints, but it also reinforces overall health.

Stretching

Stretching is something everyone should do on a regular basis, and those with chronic back pain will benefit most from stretching the soft the muscles, ligaments, and tendons in and around the spine.

It is a fact that when motion is limited the back becomes stiff, which can result in more pain. Those who suffer from chronic back pain need to stretch regularly and perform appropriate stretching movements to benefit from the sustained and long-term relief from the increased motion.

One top recommendation for dealing with chronic pain is by getting regular exercise. Exercise will help with different types of pain - from helping with arthritis by getting your body moving, to boosting your mood, when you have pain from Crohn's disease or fibromyalgia.

Yoga For Chronic Pain

Yoga can be defined as a practice based on harmonizing the mind, body, and soul. By practicing Yoga every day, you will not only explore your true self or your inner self, but also develop the feeling that you are one with nature and environment. Yoga aids the overall well-being of the body and focuses mainly on developing relationship with the natural world around us.

Pain is not just influenced by physical injury or illness, it is also greatly affected by our thoughts, anxiety, trauma, stress and emotions. Stress and pain are closely interrelated - you may experience pain when stressed and stress can also increase the intensity of the pain. When there is increased stress, your breathing becomes heavier, erratic and ragged. Your mood is also altered along with some tension and tightening of the muscles. These symptoms of chronic pain can even increase the toxins in the body and decrease oxygen levels.

Yoga addresses these problems effectively, as it involves the techniques of deep breathing and meditation, which helps in the absorption of much-needed oxygen and in the relaxation of mind and body. These breathing techniques ensure that the muscles of the lungs, diaphragm, back, and abdomen are fully utilized. When the muscles are loose and relaxed, they can help in releasing the built-up tension in the body and facilitate proper flow of energy throughout. Stress and anxiety levels will also be reduced gradually.

Yoga, or simple stretching, are simple practices that should be applied to everyday life to reduce the tension of stress and keep the muscles in proper working order. There are specific stretches that can focus on problem areas such as the neck or lower back. These stretches can be assigned from a personal trainer, massage therapist, or physiotherapist. Yoga can be enjoyed at home or in a studio with several other participants. There are many forms of yoga ranging from hatha yoga to hot yoga. The focus in yoga is on breath control, meditation, stretching, and balance. Not all forms of yoga are spiritual with chants and mantras, if you don't feel comfortable with that form of practice.

Exercise in general is good for chronic pain, but specific exercises, especially certain yoga positions, help to decrease some types of pain, like shoulder or neck pain.

Additionally, the relaxation techniques you will learn, can teach you how to manage the different types of chronic pain more effectively.

If you are considering trying yoga techniques for your chronic pain, you need to consider the style of yoga you will do.

While all forms of yoga can be beneficial for your body, mind and spirit, certain exercises are directed towards people who are struggling with chronic pain. There are multiple yoga poses or asanas and different stance can be used. Individuals with chronic pain should begin with a slow-paced, gentle yoga pose. Benefits of yoga include improved ability to handle stress, feeling more relaxed throughout the day and improvements in sleep quality. Studies have proven that yoga is helpful to prevent fibromyalgia, among other chronic pain conditions.

Massage Therapy

Massage therapy has become overwhelmingly popular, and rightfully so; in addition to feeling good, it has several health benefits. Massage therapy is wonderful for any type of pain, be it chronic, acute or simply from fatigue, work, and tension. There are various massage therapies available to meet all types of needs, including Shiatsu, Swedish, hot oil and deep tissue.

Massage has also been used as a natural anxiety remedy for ages; it may be as simple as rubbing your neck gently but whichever the case you are massaging it is an effective way to calm your nerves. The benefits of any massage therapy are many, including stress relief, relaxation, lowered blood pressure, lowered tension in the muscles, and it also improves deeper breathing. As the book unfolds, I will discuss therapeutic massage as a natural remedy for anxiety disorders, in this case it will be a deep and precise tool.

A skilled and trained massage therapist will know exactly what to do once the pain problem is explained. Massage also does wonders for fatigue and stress, both of which are known to increase pain and go hand in hand with arthritis and other chronic pain conditions. It can also help to calm anxiety, which often afflicts those who suffer from chronic pain.

If you can afford it, get a massage regularly - weekly or even twice per week. Physical therapists and chiropractors also offer therapeutic massage, so it may be covered under medical insurance.

There are also electronic massagers on the market that are great options. These include mobile units, which are spot massage products that target the neck or specific areas. There are also strap onto chair units that offer shiatsu for the entire back, many come with a heat option.

The most significant health benefit of massage is that it provides the sensation of touch, which is critical in both early childhood development and overall adult health. Levels of somatotropin, or human growth hormone, correlate directly with the amount of physical contact you receive.

Massage also cues relaxation in your nervous system. One of the biggest benefits of massage is that it feels great, especially if you're in pain. Nerves that carry information about the sensation of touch to the brain are more heavily myelinated than the nerves that carry information about pain, so touch information travels faster than pain information. Therefore, you instinctively rub the skin around a painful area; the touch sensation temporarily drowns out the pain sensation, and you're given a moment of relief.

Massage also feels good because it temporarily reduces muscle tension. Pressing on tight muscles lengthens them in the same way that gentle prolonged static stretching does, and after an hour or so of this manual lengthening you may stand up feeling like your muscles are made of jelly. If your massage therapist applies a great deal of pressure, your stretch reflex may be activated immediately, making you feel tight and sore soon after a massage. A good rule of thumb is that if you feel pain during a massage, you're probably going to feel some soreness afterward as well. While it can be difficult or awkward in the moment, it's better to ask your massage therapist to press more gently than to suffer the consequences. It is not necessary to apply a painful amount of pressure to reap the benefits of a massage. Moreover, if you're in pain, a deep massage can increase and prolong your pain by making your muscles tighter.

Lastly, massage temporarily softens connective tissues, which increases flexibility and range of motion. Tendons, ligaments, fascia (which surrounds, supports, and separates structures of the body), and scar tissue (which forms to heal an injury) are all made of collagen fibers arranged in varying patterns and densities. As muscles become habitually tighter and movement decreases, connective tissues also respond by tightening. Movement and heat can make these collagen structures more flexible and fluid.

For people with chronic pain, the most beneficial aspect of massage may be that it lowers stress, thereby reducing the sensation of pain and reactivity of the nervous system. However, a massage by itself is not enough to change deeply learned habitual movements or your resting level of muscle tension. The sensory awareness that can be gained through massage is valuable, but if it isn't followed by actual motor education in the form of voluntary movement, little lasting progress will be made. You must actively retrain your nervous system, and you can't do that with massage alone.

Brain Balance

First, you must make sure your brain is balanced. Without a balanced nervous system, your efforts to eliminate chronic pain will be wasted. Many things can cause brain imbalances. Most common are head injuries and exposure to electromagnetic radiation from personal wireless devices. Things that increase brain imbalance risk factors include:

- Using Bluetooth devices and cell phones, walkie talkies, using desktop and laptop computers and iPads.
- Eating processed foods that have MSG.
- Consuming drinks containing artificial sweeteners and drinking fluoridated water.
- Leading a stressful life.
- Not getting enough quality sleep.

Brain Balancing Using Affirmations

Studies show that when the thymus gland is balanced, both hemispheres of the brain also remain balanced and serve to lower chronic pain. The nice thing about affirmations is that they don't cost you anything; you just must repeat the affirmations regularly throughout the day to keep your brain in balance. You need to "feel" the words to get full benefits. The following is a list of daily affirmations:

- I have faith, gratitude, trust, love and courage.
- I'm modest, I'm humble and tolerant.
- I'm clean and good, I deserve to be loved.
- I'm content and tranquil.
- I have forgiveness in my heart.
- My life energy is high, life is full of love.

Brain Balancing Music

Brain balancing music encourages a balanced nervous system and balances both hemispheres of the brain. Brain balancing music uses three coordinated methods: "primordial sounds", "brainwave entrainment", and "multi-layered music" to bring the mind-body into a deeply relaxed and balanced state. You must listen to the music daily to maintain your brain balance which is crucial for health and healing of chronic pain.

Avoid GMO foods

GMO or genetically modified organisms have been introduced to our diets over the past decade. As of this writing, the GMO foods are not labeled in the U. S. So, the average American's is unconsciously consuming GMO rich canola oil, sugar. beets, corn, soy and cottonseed oil. GMO foods can cause all sorts of gastrointestinal problems, allergies, weight gain, and immune problems. Avoiding GMO foods can reduce or even eliminate many health problems, including chronic pain.

Emotional Freedom Techniques

This amazing technique deals swiftly with all sorts of emotional pain and has an infinite number of applications. EFT has been around for quite a while and is now used in many hospitals and psych units throughout the world by professional psychologists and psychiatrists who are continuing to get very positive results with severe emotional pain and trauma.

There is no doubt that strong emotions can be very painful things and it is now recognized that emotion follows thought. Therefore, psychiatrists spend years talking about trauma and trying to uncover triggers and thoughts that cause bad feelings, depression, phobias and the like.

EFT is a great way to deal with all fear though you will have to be thorough. Really look at all the different aspects of that fear and treat each one with a very specific opening statement.

Emotional Freedom Technique (EFT) or tapping requires that you tap specific acupressure points on the torso, hands and on the head in order to clear energy blocks caused by negative emotions and feelings.

What you do is tap lightly on each of them. You get used to doing this very quickly, and when you have been using EFT for a while you can just do a few taps here and there, maybe on your collarbone or under your eye, for rapid relief.

Generally tapping involves two stages. In the first stage you are tapping to express the negative emotions. This stage of tapping will last if you have an emotional charge, continual tapping will bring that charge down to a minimal level.

The second stage includes reframing the condition positively where you choose a positive emotion or thought to replace the negative ones. The cool thing is you can't tap incorrectly; your intention is enough to make it work correctly. Even without tapping the right acupressure points, you will still release the negative energy from your body.

Step by Step Instructions to Strengthen your Vagus Nerve to Upgrade Your Whole Body

The vagal pathway is an arrangement of nerves that interfaces outward from the cerebrum and directs numerous organs in the body – the heart, lungs, gut, liver and more

The current drug regards singular organs as the zone of illness and disregards the way that your mind and sensory system instruct your organs. Your organs normally send a status check to your cerebrum through the vagus nerve to give an account of how things are going.

It's a two-way road. When everything's working out in a good way, your cerebrum keeps up business as usual. At the point when an organ is battling, it can move toward your cerebrum for more assets. At the point when it's the ideal opportunity for your body to spring to activity, your vagus nerve conveys the sign from your cerebrum to your organs to back off.

To ensure nothing is lost in interpretation, your vagus nerve should be in working request. Your mind and organs rely upon your vagal pathways to control things like:

- Yearning hormones and nourishment intake
- Inflammation
- Nervousness and fight-or-flight
- The safe response

Since the vagus nerves are associated with so a lot, it must be working appropriately. Peruse on to discover how you can bolster your vagus nerve using vagal conditioning.

It's cliché, but take deep breaths

There's an association between breath and pulse, which is adjusted by the vagus nerve. That's the reason ordinary yoga practice diminishes by and large stress.

Yoga breathing and guided breathing activities, quiet your pulse and lower your blood pressure. Breathing activities expanded vagal tone and successfully oversaw prehypertension in an exploratory group.

In one examination, slow breathing activities improved autonomic capacities in sound members. Quick breathing didn't. That's since quick breathing makes your body believe you're running from predators. That sets off your body's alerts and initiates a pressure reaction.

Box breathing for s.o.s.

In case you're terrified or going to blow a gasket, attempt box relaxing.

1. Breathe in for a check of four.
2. Hold for a check of four.
3. Breathe out for a check of four.
4. Sit tight for a check of four.
5. Rehash until your hands are back on the controls.

A primary couple of times, follow your finger in a square example noticeable all around. It'll assist you with recollecting how to do it when you're fatigued.

The slow development of your lungs signs to your heart to back off, which sends a sentiment of quiet all through your whole sensory system. Your vagus nerve associates the entirety of this flagging and discharges acetylcholine, a quieting synthetic you can give yourself a fix of whenever by doing unwinding systems.

Relax, LITERALLY

Becoming acclimated to the virus conditions the vagus reaction, which eases back the actuation of the thoughtful sensory system. Customary virus impacts quantifiably lessen pressure markers. Cold presentation calmed indications of sorrow and uneasiness perhaps balanced by the vagus nerve. Invigorating the vagal pathways animates digestion. When rodents' absorption eased back down because of tension, cold introduction re-enacted the gastric nerves and got everything moving once more. Everything occurred through vagal pathways.

Keep your gut happy

Have you ever known about the gut-cerebrum pivot? That alludes to the microorganisms in your stomach related framework speaking with your mind.

Your microbiome is the biological system of well-disposed microorganisms in your body and on your skin. Regularly, when somebody discusses the microbiome, they're discussing the microorganisms in your digestion tracts and colon.

As the study of the microbiome fabricates, established researchers investigate an ever-increasing number of ways the microbiome influences your whole body.

Research on the association between the microbiome and temperament is extending, and correspondence among gut and mind relies on — shock — the vagus nerve.

Concentrates on creature models and people bolster the possibility that a flourishing microbiome controls tension and improves your state of mind. A portion of the exploration analyzed this impact with and without an unblemished vagus nerve, to check whether vagal pathways have anything to do with it.

Rats who enhanced with specific strains of probiotics demonstrated declines in uneasiness and discouragement pointers, however not in creatures whose vagus nerves were cut before the experiment.

Specialists see the useful impacts of probiotics on temperament in humans. Healthy ladies who ate aged nourishments for about a month demonstrated positive changes in mind movement, especially in the pieces of the cerebrum that control feeling and sensation From the creature examines, and from what researchers think about the vagus nerve as of now, you can make a strong conjecture that the gut-mind correspondence here occurs through the vagus nerve. An ideal approach to help your intestinal vegetation is to get a thorough microbiome test like Viome. Viome is a test-at-home pack that you use to profile your microbiome effectively, and afterward, you get customized dietary proposals to bring you once again into balance.

Discover your safety cues

Vagus nerve master Dr. Stephen Porges built up Polyvagal Theory (more on that on a scene of Bulletproof Radio), which spreads out a choice procedure of sorts that decides if battle or-flight actuates. You are not aware of this procedure — everything occurs out of sight, and various parts of the vagus nerve actuate because of various circumstances.

At the point when you experience an alarming improvement, the principal layer to traverse is the one that reacts to social correspondence — verbal language, non-verbal communication, vocal tone, and other nonverbal cues. If the upgrade is too solid even to consider reasoning through, your mind initiates the battle or flight reaction. At the point when that falls flat, the crudest dread reaction is feigning unconsciousness — feeling solidified.

At the point when you realize your dread is unreasonable, you can utilize wellbeing prompts to stop alarm at the main layer and prevent your cerebrum from finding a workable pace or-flight reaction. Here are a few things you can attempt.

Utilize soothing voices

In his meeting on Bulletproof Radio, Stephen Porges clarifies one way this marvel is designed in kids. Youngsters are quantifiably quieted by prosodic (sing-song) talking, otherwise called "mothers'." Waldorf schools train instructors to embrace this tone to keep up a quiet and cheerful study hall. If you've visited your local play area in the first part of the day, you've seen it in real life.

Modifying your tone of discourse works for grown-ups, as well. Guided reflections, either face to face or recorded, receive a moderate, musical tone of talking. Utilizing the voice as an unwinding signal persuades your cerebrum into a casual state quicker than an ordinary conversational tone would.

Train your safety cues

With a little practice, you can prepare your psyche to have a sense of security. Wellbeing signs prevent your dread and tension reactions from kicking in.

One approach to do this is to make your "sheltered spot" or "upbeat spot" while you're quiet. To do this, you envision you're at a spot where you're calm and feeling content and quiet. Use as a lot of tangible data as you can – envision the sights, smells, sounds, and so forth.

Practice this representation frequently. That way, when you start feeling dreadful or irate, you can start the "protected spot" absent a lot of exertion. It's there when you need it.

Deal with YOUR MYELIN

Your vagus nerve is myelinated, which implies it's canvassed in a defensive covering of fat that protects it and enables the signs to go through effectively. At the point when myelin on any nerve separates, the nerve doesn't fill in too. Peruse this post to become familiar with how to adore your myelin.

Precisely IMPLANTED ELECTRICAL VAGUS NERVE STIMULATOR

The vagus nerve initiates the insusceptible framework when you're battling something. Doctors utilize this information for treatment by invigorating the vagus nerve with power and pharmaceuticals to treat provocative disorders. Doctors precisely embed electric vagus nerve triggers in patients with extreme epilepsy or discouragement since it hoses the aggravation response.

YOU CAN TONE YOUR BABY'S VAGUS NERVE

A few elements play into the infant's vagal tone. Children who are brought into the world untimely or destined to moms who had discouragement and uneasiness during pregnancy have a low vagal tone.

If you were experiencing a few things during pregnancy, don't stress. You can help tone your child's vagal pathways with typical holding practices and cherishing care.

Cold showers ought to likely hold up until junior is mature enough to consent to it. During the infant years, newborn child back rub and kangaroo care (holding infant skin-to-skin) help children's vagal tone develop. If your children are past the infant organize, you can work with them on a portion of the adult approaches to condition the vagus nerve, such as breathing procedures and cold impacts in the shower. A back rub, a yoga class, and a couple of moments of goosebumps in the shower are presumably justified, despite all the trouble thinking about that the advantages of vagal nerve conditioning stretch out to each significant organ in your body and back. For more approaches to help your entire framework, head-to-toe, pop your data into the crate underneath, so you don't miss a thing.

Is there a role for vagus nerve stimulation in the treatment of posttraumatic stress disorder?

Posttraumatic stress disorder (PTSD) creates in people who have been presented to injury and subsequently languish trouble or practical debilitation over at any multi rate-month. Side effects incorporate sentiments of re-encountering the horrendous mishap, staying away from tokens of the injury, elevated nervousness and excitement, and negative contemplations or emotions. Ongoing cataclysmic events, mass shootings, militant psychological assaults, and urban areas under attack add to the worldwide weight of PTSD which, as indicated by a recent report, influences 4–6% of the worldwide populace, although most of the injuries are identified with mishaps and sexual or physical savagery. Shockingly, there is no known fix, and flow medicines are not compelling for all patients. A PTSD psychopharmacology working gathering as of late distributed their accord articulation calling for a quick activity to address the emergency in PTSD treatment, referring to three significant concerns. In the first place, just two medications (sertraline and paroxetine) are affirmed by the US FDA for the treatment of PTSD. These prescriptions diminish manifestation seriousness; however, they may not deliver total abatement of side effects. The subsequent concern is identified with polypharmacy. PTSD patients are recommended meds to address every one of their numerous one of a kind and various indications including tension, trouble resting, sexual brokenness, despondency, and constant torment, with inadequate experimental examinations of medication collaborations. The high comorbidity among PTSD and dependence gives further difficulties to pharmacotherapies. The third significant concern is the absence of progressions in the treatment of PTSD; no new drugs have been endorsed since 2001.

Going past indication alleviation, the 'highest quality level' injury centered way to deal with treating PTSD pathology is presentation-based treatment, where patients are presented to the tokens of the injury until they figure out how to connect these signs with security. Although there is acceptable proof for adequacy with this methodology, not all patients completely react to the treatment. Exposure treatment relies upon the way toward stifling the adapted dread memory, which is overwhelmed by another memory that creates through rehashed exposures. The patients with uneasiness issues and PTSD show disabilities in their capacity to smother molded feelings of fear, which could add to the advancement of clutters and may meddle with progress in treatment. Since the memory of the injury isn't lost in any case, rather, enhancements through treatment rely upon newly learned affiliations that horrible rival affiliations, the parity of the two recollections can move after some time, prompting backslide. Different difficulties remember the trouble for perceiving and dousing apprehension of every single molded improvement, and a high dropout rate, which isn't astounding given that evasion is one of the side effects of PTSD.

Numerous creatures investigate labs have put forth attempts to create adjunctive medicines to quicken or upgrade the impacts of presentation-based treatments. Spearheading work did by Michael Davis indicated that organization of the psychological improving medication d-cycloserine before presenting rodents to unreinforced adapted signs upgraded annihilation, and he and his associates along these lines deciphered the disclosure when they found that d-cycloserine additionally upgraded the impacts of presentation treatment in patients with explicit fears. Notwithstanding, aftereffects of studies surveying the impacts of psychological enhancers as subordinates to presentation treatment are blended on account of PTSD. A potential clarification is that medications given before introduction treatment sessions risk fortifying negative affiliations if presentation produces uneasiness. Anxiolytic medications have been attempted because of proof that these medications ought to improve decency and lessen the nervousness reaction during the introduction. In any case, results show that anxiolytic medications don't upgrade the impacts of introduction treatment. One clarification is that the uneasiness reaction is required for accomplishment in presentation treatment since patients must learn not to fear their fear reaction. On the other hand, similarly, as stress can upgrade the capacity of horrendous accidents, the nervousness reaction may improve the solidification of the eradication memory. Predictable with this, anxiolytic medications will, in general, hinder memory union. A perfect extra would take advantage of the systems that upgrade the solidification of horrible recollections to advance eradication recollections that are similarly as solid, at the same time bypassing or staying away from the aversive pressure reaction.

Developing proof proposes that vagus nerve stimulation (VNS) might be an advantageous extra to introduction-based treatments through its explicit blending improvement of memory union and neural pliancy. Enthusiasm for the vagus nerve (the tenth cranial nerve) as a neuromodulator originates from a very long while of research showing that the vagus nerve fills in as a scaffold between the fringe autonomic sensory system and the cerebrum. It flags the cerebrum during times of elevated thoughtful action, advancing quick stockpiling of recollections that are significant for endurance. As a component of the parasympathetic nervous system, the actuation of the vagus nerve neutralizes the thoughtful pressure reaction.

VNS improves memory in rats and people, proposing that blending VNS with the unreinforced presentation to adapted signals may upgrade the solidification of the termination memory. Reliable with this speculation, we found that VNS upgraded the elimination of molded fear in rats. Broad proof demonstrates that VNS advances neural pliancy, particularly when it is combined with preparing, and this impact includes VNS tweak of the locus coeruleus noradrenergic framework. We have watched versatility impacts in the eradication related infralimbic prefrontal cortex – basolateral amygdala pathway in the wake of matching VNS with an introduction to unreinforced adapted signs, proposing that VNS-upgraded annihilation might be vigorous, dependable, and less helpless to backslide. In an ongoing report, we found that VNS additionally improved the eradication of adapted dread in a rodent model of PTSD. These rodents express a considerable lot of the biomarkers and social phenotypes that are related to PTSD and, critically, they are impervious to termination of adapted fear. We found that the VNS organization during elimination sessions turned around this eradication disability and forestalled the arrival of dread. VNS-treated rodents likewise performed better on trial of tension, excitement, shirking, and social cooperation's multi-week later, showing that inversion of the term disability meant enhancements in other PTSD manifestations.

Furthermore, interminable, unpaired VNS, as is utilized in the treatment of epilepsy and misery, improved execution on the Hamilton Anxiety Scale in certain patients with uneasiness issue, and decreased nervousness like conduct in rats. The impacts of VNS on annihilation in our examinations are not seen when the VNS is controlled 30 min to 1 h in the wake of preparing. Subsequently, VNS alone isn't adequate to diminish the dread reaction. These discoveries propose that VNS may diminish nervousness, however matching explicit versatility and memory adjustment is essential for eradication upgrade. Our ongoing, unpublished discoveries demonstrate that rodents are bound to investigate the open arms of a raised in addition to labyrinth following accepting VNS, recommending that VNS produces an intense anxiolytic impact. Moreover, corticosterone levels expanded altogether in hoax treated rodents following testing on the raised in addition to labyrinth, yet such an expansion was not seen in VNS-treated rodents. This work ought to be reproduced in different settings, however it is an empowering initial move toward recognizing an aide treatment that may improve pass ableness and viability in presentation-based treatments.

Conclusion

Your diet is going to facilitate just about everything in your body. If your body does not have the nutrients that it needs, it will not be able to function properly, and you will find that you do not properly manage to produce the right stimulation and tone that you need. You must ensure that your vagus nerve has the support that it needs to support your entire body if you want to be able to rely on it, and that will primarily come from diet.

You will find that omega-3 fatty acids will be a great addition to your diet. This is not only healthy for your brain; it is good for your nerves as well. It will help you facilitate all sorts of healthy neuronal connections that will then allow the vagus nerve to work the way that it is supposed to. You may try to add fatty fish to your diet to help meet this need, for example—you may choose to eat salmon or tuna. However, be mindful of the fact that seafood can oftentimes come along with mercury, so try to eat fish with lower mercury content whenever you can.

Beyond that, you will want to eat a wide range of foods as often as you can. You will want to ensure that you are eating healthy fruits and vegetables to aid in digestion and support your body properly. When you eat plenty of fruits and vegetables, especially fibrous ones, you will be directly supporting your gut bacteria, giving them the proper nutrition that they need to function. Beyond just that, everyone should be eating a rainbow every day—try to make sure that the foods that you eat cover the entire spectrum of colors for optimal digestion and health.

Along those same lines, you want to make sure that you support the vagus nerve by ensuring that you have healthy gut bacteria present. Remember, the vagus nerve primarily deals with this area of the body—it is responsible for making sure that you are getting the food you need, and your gut bacteria will alter it. The bacteria in your digestive tract plays more of a role than just digesting your food—it also creates neurotransmitters, and it has been found that anxiety and depression can be related back to having a poor balance of gut bacteria in the first place. If you realize that your gut bacteria are out of sorts, you probably are currently suffering from either digestive issues or you have noticed that your mood is not what it used to be. No matter the reason or why you feel the way that you do, it is important for you to stop and think that maybe you should try treating the gut with probiotics.

You will want to find probiotics that are rich in both lactobacillus Rhamnosus and Bifidobacterium Longum. These two bacteria strains have been found to improve vagus nerve function while also reducing stress hormone production within animals. By making sure that you are taking a probiotic on a regular basis, you will likely see an improvement in your mood.

Exercise is another crucial step in ensuring that your vagus nerve stays healthy. Your vagus nerve is connected to just about every part of your vital organs. It is innervating your heart and lungs, which both get a workout when you are exercising yourself. This means that you are naturally training your vagus nerve at the same time. When you use your vagus nerve on the regular, you will find that you are beginning to see those changes in behaviors that you need. When you exercise, you will tone your heart, your breathing, and even your vagus nerve.

When you want to exercise your vagus nerve, you will be wanting to look for exercises that will either stretch the chest and abdominal muscles to directly strengthen the vagus nerve through direct stimulation, or you will want to use cardio exercise to get the heart pumping and the blood moving. When you do so on the regular, your vagus nerve will have to engage regularly. You can see that the vagus nerve activates more as well with how the time that it takes your body to recover from this stress quickly begins to dwindle. Because it will get so used to activating on the regular, you will find that it is commonly growing stronger and more active in general, which is good news for you. The stronger your vagus nerve, the better your emotional regulation and health will become.

Finally, we are going to look at social relationships and your vagus nerve. When you are socializing with someone else, your vagus nerve is already active. It is activating the social engagement system—the part of your brain that is entirely interested in interacting more with those around you. When you activate this part of your brain, you usually find that you are calmer in general. You will literally be triggering the activity of the "tend and befriend" mode of your brain. This is important—when you look at this part of the brain, you begin to realize something: You are using your vagus nerve.

This makes sense. When you consider that the vagus nerve passes through the face, and the vagus nerve facilitates emotional regulation, you would think that it would be strongly related to how likely or how little you want to socialize with other people. When you activate this system within the brain, you are happier to work with other people. You are open to communication and more likely to be smiling and happy in general.

What is interesting, however, is the fact that many social activities also activate the vagus nerve as well. A good, long laugh with someone else is going to be triggering the vagus nerve as well. It does this through a few different methods. Firstly, you must consider that laughing is loud. When you laugh with someone else, you are likely to laugh deeper and louder. Laughing also forces you to take big, deep breaths, which will also engage the vagus nerve. Beyond that, however, you will also see that you are smiling. Smiling is yet another way that you can trigger your vagus nerve to activate as well, thanks to the fact that it innervates all those muscles. Essentially, just being social with other people is enough for you to stimulate the vagus nerve and kick it into action. When you do this, you will find that you are much more likely to facilitate it growing healthier and stronger.

As you can see, there are several different life choices that you can make that will sort of support the development of the vagus nerve. When you have a healthy social life, you are much more likely to laugh regularly. You are much more likely to smile and facilitate a good, strong social engagement response. When you eat well and use probiotics, you ensure that you have the proper microbiota to deal with what your body needs to do as well as to make sure that you are getting all sorts of good neurotransmitters produced within your body. When you stop and make sure that you are exercising, you directly train your vagus nerve as well.

Beyond just training the vagus nerve, however, you may notice that all four of those choices that you can make will also facilitate a healthier lifestyle in general. You will be healthier physically and mentally, not only because of the vagus nerve but also because you have made the healthy choices that your body needed.

CPSIA information can be obtained
at www.ICGtesting.com
Printed in the USA
BVHW071355270421
605946BV00002B/429